LIVING ON THE
PLUS SIDE

Brownlow Publishing Company, Inc.
6309 Airport Freeway
Fort Worth, Texas 76117

LIVING ON THE PLUS SIDE

Biblical Answers to Strengthen Your Family's Finances

Leroy Brownlow

BROWNLOW PUBLISHING COMPANY, INC.

CONTENTS

Foreword

GOD WANTS MAN to prosper. This is clearly spelled out by the apostle John in his letter to Gaius: "I wish above all things *that thou mayest prosper* and be in health, even as thy soul prospereth" (III John 2). To know that our Maker wants us to live on the plus side of life and that He cares about our welfare is very encouraging and motivating.

Wanting the human family to prosper, God provided a world of abundant blessings for man's sustenance and enjoyment, and calls it "very good" (Genesis 1:28-31). And what God calls *good* man should not call *bad*.

Truly, man's very nature — a creature in the image of God, a little lower than the angels — befits a proud birth and a life of plenty. To think otherwise contradicts the design of all the earth. Hence, *man the best of God's creation should not be expected to have only a skimpy, wolf-at-the-door existence.*

Not only has the Creator arranged it so man can have the best in a world of blessings: He has gone further and even given the rules or conditions whereby man may attain these blessings. And in this volume those prerequisites are pointed out and discussed. They are basic. They are unerring. They can change a person's whole economic future. If you follow them, you are sure to prosper.

While financial success meets one of man's needs, it is certainly not the whole of life. This was plainly stated by Jesus in the well known words: "Man shall not live by bread alone, but by every word that proceedeth out of the mouth of God" (Matthew 4:4). However, we further note that Jesus did suggest in the passage that man does live by bread — but not by bread only. Thus, His words definitely signify two needs of man — physical and spiritual — and one does not take the place of the other.

Believing that man is born to have — it is his birthright — the author wishes you true success, the best of two worlds, now and later.

— Leroy Brownlow

ONE

God and Money

MANY PEOPLE ARE perplexed concerning prosperity. They want it, but they have erroneously thought that God did not want them to have it and to enjoy it. Yet, the Bible says: "I wish above all things that thou mayest prosper" (III John 2). And "God who giveth us richly all things to enjoy" (I Timothy 6:17). Despite these Scriptures some have mistakenly thought that God doesn't like for us to have money, that He actually hates it and is against it.

This attitude, though wrong, has grown quite naturally and can be explained. From our youth, many of us learned to quote the following passages:

> No man can serve two masters: for either he will hate the one, and love the other, or else he will hold to the one, and despise the other. Ye cannot serve God and mammon.
>
> Matthew 6:24

> For the love of money is the root of all evil.
>
> I Timothy 6:10

From these verses, many have mistakenly concluded that: (1) If you love God, you must hate money, and that (2) God says money is evil, which He does not say. This notion has had a voice throughout church history, and some have even equated godliness with poverty. Yet, they openly admit that poverty is one of the greatest evils in the world today. The paradox is very glaring.

It is evident that confusion prevails in the minds of many. Hence, this study is highly appropriate. What is God's attitude toward money and wealth and riches? Can we please God and have material possessions? We need honest answers. Perhaps we have failed to get a balanced approach to this subject. We have diligently taught good stewardship, but we have never done much teaching on God's principles for making and saving money. If He has some teachings on the topic and we have not taught them, then we can hardly say that we have declared "all the counsel of God" (Acts 20:27). *A very definite responsibility!* This truism should be considered: Unless God's people make and save finances, they will never have any to give to His causes throughout the world.

God knows more about money than we do. He knows its strengths and weaknesses, its helps and its hurts, its blessings and its curses. Wealth is a little like fire. Both are basically *amoral* and can be used for good or evil. When once we understand the dangers of fire, we can use it for tremendous blessings. So it is with wealth.

Happily, we are not left to wonder or speculate how much a person can prosper materially without endangering himself. The Bible gives us this infallible measurement:

> Beloved, I wish above all things that thou mayest prosper and be in health, even as thy soul prospereth.
>
> III John 2

That tells us how long one can prosper materially with

no peril to him — *just as long as his soul prospers.* Just that long — whether he has little or much — it can be helpful and fill a divinely ordained need. For it does not have him, he has it.

The major purposes of living are to be happy, to help others, to walk humbly with God and to be eternally saved. "For what shall it profit a man, if he shall gain the whole world, and lose his own soul" (Mark 8:36)? Anything that alters this conception of life is detrimental.

Let us therefore understand that there is a big difference between *Financial Accumulation* and *Financial Success.* In the last analysis, success is that which helps and blesses, meaning that true financial success is the possession of wealth that aids one, his family, others and good causes. If not, why have it? Otherwise, the accumulator has spent his time in the vain quest of that which has no meaning, shortly endures and mocks him in the end.

So let us be aware that wealth is hard to acquire and even harder to use wisely.

Now we note some dangers of wealth and conditions which nullify its value and render it nonsuccess and a miscarriage of the purpose for which God has provided it:

1. There is no success in having a bankroll, if one is possessed with the love of it.

> For the love of money is the root of all evil: which while some coveted after, they have erred from the faith, and pierced themselves through with many sorrows.
>
> I Timothy 6:10

Sorrows, not joys! In the passage the apostle gets to the core of the problem, which is not money but the *love* of money that traps people "into temptation and a snare, and into many foolish and hurtful lusts, which drown men in destruction and perdition" (I Timothy 6:9).

So let us see the real evil: The Bible does not picture money as injurious; it is the *love* of money that the Bible condemns. Money itself can be good or bad, depending on how it is held and the use that is made of it. The fact that it can be misused does not indict it as being evil. All good things can be perverted and used to hurt. Even a pulpit can be employed to preach false doctrine instead of truth. A Sunday School class, a Sunday School picnic, a ball game, a charity offering and a thousand other good things can be misused and made harmful. So let us not confuse the issue. Furthermore, may we not be inconsistent: condemn money as evil and then pass the contribution plates at church to get a little more "evil."

Neither let us err in thinking that the apostle's condemnation of the love of money applies to only large sums. To love a dollar is as sinful as to love a million. It is not the amount involved but the love of it that is wrong. So this rebuke falls equally hard on both the rich and the poor, for some of the poor indisputably love money as much as some of the rich — just not as prosperous.

2. Neither is any person who idolizes wealth a financial success, even though a materialistically impressed society may regard him as such. For one to make the Almighty Dollar his god is but to pervert the purpose

of wealth and to injure himself. Indeed, covetousness is
a form of idolatry.

> . . . and covetousness, which is idolatry.
>
> Colossians 3:5

However, money does not qualify as deity. There is
only one God, the Eternal Spirit and the Father of our
being. And there are not to be any other gods. No, not
materialism. In the basic rules of living — Ten Commandments — this is made plain:

> Thou shalt have no other gods before me.
>
> Exodus 20:3

Knowing the absolute necessity of this, our illustrious
forefathers printed on our money, IN GOD WE TRUST.
As long as our trust is in Him our days are excellent,
for this within itself is the most beneficial of all at-
tainments. On the other hand, when wealth rather than
God commands, ills fare the day. In the same vein we
hear the famous British statesman and author:

> *If we command our wealth, we shall be rich and free.*
> *If our wealth command us, we are poor indeed.*
>
> *Edmund Burke*

Unquestionably, any person who trusts in riches and
is wedded to them is in a difficult condition to go to
heaven. Jesus said, "A rich man shall hardly [with dif-
ficulty] enter into the kingdom of heaven" (Matthew
19:23). Lest we be confused, let us keep in mind the
following facts pertaining to what Jesus said:

First, wealth is a relative thing. The poorest in
America are considered rich according to the standard
used by some other people in the world.

Second, the rich man in the context of whom Jesus was speaking loved and trusted in riches more than God, which he demonstrated on that occasion. In Mark's account of this particular rich man's conduct and the teachings of Jesus, we are given this clarification: "Children, how hard is it for them that trust in riches to enter into the kingdom of God" (Mark 10:24). Note the word "trust" in the passage, for it is a key word in ascertaining the real meaning of what Jesus taught. It is not the man that is rich but the man that *trusts* in riches that has a seeming impossibility of going to heaven.

Third, Jesus next stated, "It is easier for a camel to go through the eye of a needle, than for a rich man to enter into the kingdom of heaven." Such hyperboles were and are customary in all languages, and Jesus used this one. It shows impossibility, yet Jesus stated that "with God all things are possible." A fundamental of salvation is: No man can save himself by himself; and to be shaken from such a state of self-independence and earthly trust to a recognition of one's spiritual bankruptcy is all the harder for the rich man. So, the *impossibility* is a contingent thing that is overcome by appealing to the help of God. When one wins the battle of trusting in the right One instead of the wrong thing, it is then that he is prepared to receive the words of salvation, and then that which seems impossible is made possible. It happened to the rich man Zaccheus (Luke 19:1-9). And what happened to him can happen to any person who meets the condition.

3. Nor is there success in financial accumulation, if it makes one high-minded. Two specific commands to the

rich in this world are that they not be proud and that they not trust in riches:

> Charge them that are rich in this world, that they be not high-minded, nor trust in uncertain riches, but in the living God who giveth us richly all things to enjoy.
>
> I Timothy 6:17

Only God is certain! Riches are not!

Most assuredly, the person who gathers some of this world's goods has no cause for pride. Really, it is to the glory of God and not man. In the first place, the blessings come form God: it is His world with all its blessings. "Every good gift and every perfect gift is from above, and cometh down from the Father of lights . . ." (James 1:17). Our recognition of the true source of wealth is humbling.

4. Furthermore, one is not financially successful unless he enjoys what he has. God meant for us to enjoy His blessings: ". . . the living God who giveth us richly all things to enjoy" (I Timothy 6:17). The passage tells us the purpose of having — "to enjoy." It is right. It is divine. Remember — God is the giver: therefore, let us trust in the Giver, not in the gifts. Obviously, this is the best way to live: trust in God for it is peaceful; enjoy His blessings for it is pleasurable. Peace and pleasure — two divinely appointed benefits for man. But if we do not enjoy the blessings God has provided, then we have frustrated His design in giving them. Lest there be a miscarriage of God's plans let us be aware that —

> *Wealth is not his that has it, but his that enjoys it.*
> *Italian Proverb*

Consequently, *there are three fundamental problems concerning wealth:* first, *get it;* second, *enjoy it;* and, third, *use it to aid others and good works.* Only the wisest succeed at the latter two.

5. Likewise, there is no more pitiable nonattainment than the affluent person who has allowed wealth to make a dissipating fool of him. Maybe Kin Hubbard put it a better way: "Money never made a fool of anybody; it only shows 'em up." Anyway, a fool and money are sometimes seen together. Even Jesus called a certain rich man a fool, not because he was rich but for other reasons (Luke 12:13-21). If abundance goes to a man's head, there has to be an empty place there; and what a misusage if it projects him faster and more furiously down the disappointing road of debauchery. So money in the hands of some is an awful curse.

> *Abundance is the blessing of the wise;*
> *The use of riches in discretion lies;*
> *Learn this, ye men of wealth: a heavy purse*
> *In a fool's pocket is a heavy curse.*
>
> *From the Greek*

May we never forget: It takes more intelligence and greater virtue to handle prosperity than poverty.

6. Also a fortune gained dishonestly is another colossal, financial nonsuccess. And mean, too! One of the essential ingredients of economic triumph has ever been:

> Defraud not.
>
> Mark 10:19

There is no victory in anything, if you cheat. Definitely not in the game of finance. To be a winner, you have to win according to the rules. There is no accomplishment in filling a bank with dishonest dollars.

> *Didst thou never hear that things ill got had ever bad success?*
>
> *William Shakespeare*

7. Another way a person can hold wealth in failure is to permit it to choke out the Word of God in his heart. Jesus warned of this in the Parable of the Sower:

> He also that received seed among the thorns is he that heareth the word; and the care of this world, and the deceitfulness of riches, choke the word, and he becometh unfruitful.
>
> Matthew 13:22

You will recall that in your yard a stronger grass chokes out the weaker strain. Similarily, if man's obsession for riches is stronger than his desire for the Word, then the Word will be choked out.

The verse declares that riches are deceitful. Many have been fooled. It happened because they lost sight of the more valuable things in life. Sorrowfully, they later learned that money could not buy the most treasured values in the world.

But the gold does not deceive anybody unless he permits it. Job is proof of this. Riches never choked the Word in his heart. Neither did financial collapse. Though Job had experienced abundant wealth, he disclaimed any wrong connection with it. He rather soul-searchingly stated: "If I have made gold my hope [he had not], or have said to the fine gold, Thou art my confidence [he did not]; if I rejoiced because my wealth was great, and because mine hand had gotten much" (Job 31:23,24). No, gold was not the hub of his life nor his greatest joy. God was. Consequently, materialism never replaced spirituality in his life.

8. Additionally, one is headed for disappointment if he expects riches to satisfy all needs. Never has. Because man's needs go deeper than materials. "Man shall not live by bread alone" (Matthew 4:4). The very nature of man cries out for something that materials cannot satisfy.

Furthermore, the person who loves wealth can never get enough to satisfy. Solomon stated it correctly:

> He that loveth silver shall not be satisfied with silver; nor he that loveth abundance with increase: this is also vanity.
>
> Ecclesiastes 5:10

To amass riches for only the purpose of piling them up is "vanity, yea, it is a sore travil" (Ecclesiastes 4:8). Solomon talks about "a time to get" and "a time to keep," and enunciates the principles that will resolve man's economic problems (Proverbs; Ecclesiastes), yet he also rebukes as vanity the gathering of wealth just for the sake of piling it up. In such a case, what a useless pile!

So — if your only standard of success is spelled $UCCE$$, then you are really a sad failure.

9. Furthermore, financial success becomes a catastrophe, if one thinks his soul can live on earthly wealth. Sadly, this was the foolish futility of one of the rich men spoken of in the Bible. After reaping a bountiful harvest that exceeded the capacity of his barns, he resolved: "This will I do: I will pull down my barns, and build greater; and there will I bestow all my fruits and my goods. And I will say to my soul, Soul, thou hast much goods laid up for many years; take thine ease, eat, drink and be merry" (Luke 12:18,19).

However, the loss of all was just minutes away. Thus "God said unto him, Thou fool [and a big one], this night thy soul shall be required of thee: then whose shall those things be, which thou hast provided?" Realistically, when the pale horse gallops your way, how useless is a barn full of goods.

This rich man was not dishonest. Not a criminal. No ravager of society. No meddler in other people's business. To the contrary, he had many worthy things going for him: energetic, thrifty, organized and ambitious, but to no real avail, for he thought his soul could live on stuff stacked in a barn. It cannot! Because man has a hunger that nothing material can satisfy.

10. Summed up, prosperity that is allowed to hurt a person in any manner, temporally or eternally, is a misfortune. It is a case of having wealth to one's disadvantage, the unsuccess of which is rightly pointed out by Solomon:

> There is a sore evil which I have seen under the sun,
> namely, riches kept for the owners thereof to their hurt.
>
> Ecclesiastes 5:13

The man who penned this was not against wealth; instead, he was one of the richest men of all times. What he was against is wealth that enslaves and harms. Both Scripture and observation tell us that wealth can be an enormous blessing or a terrible curse, depending upon the possessor's attitude toward it and use of it.

THINK ON THESE THINGS

1. What are three fundamental problems concerning wealth?
2. How can riches be deceitful?
3. What is your concept of financial success?
4. Why have many people thought God hated money?
5. In what way are fire and money similar?
6. What are some of the dangers of wealth?
7. How long can a person be financially prosperous and pleasing to God at the same time?
8. Are you prepared to handle wealth?

The Meaning of Family Financial Success

A FEW YEARS ago a man who came to me for a consultation asked this question, along with others: "How would you define or what would you say is the meaning of financial success?" I told him that it embraces too much and has too many ramifications to be reduced to a simple statement. However, in our short interview I did briefly mention some of the thoughts in this chapter and some in the first chapter.

Believing the inquirer's question is of common interest to us all, I now present more and broader answers. It is essential to a full discussion of *Living on the Plus Side.* For we must first understand what it is.

1. Clearly, it is a material state for the sustenance, protection and enjoyment of the physical man. It is earthly, something that belongs to this world. It is a state not given to angels, to those who have no material wants. It was given to humans, and they have physical needs as well as spiritual ones. Indeed, the spiritual part of man is more important than the physical, but this does not lessen the needs of the physical; and this takes us into the realm of food, shelter, clothing, health and security in old age. This is real! And no amount of emotionalism will alter the rationalism of meeting this need.

While it is true that Jesus said, "Man shall not live

by bread alone" (Matthew 4:4), it is also true that His words do suggest that *man does live on bread* (but not on bread only), and to this need we address ourselves in this book.

2. Truly, it concerns the basic instinct of survival. The inbred urge to survive has a very pronounced bearing on man's behavior. It made a farmer out of Cain and a shepherd out of Abel (Genesis 4:2), a fisherman out of Peter (Matthew 4:18), a merchant out of Lydia (Acts 16:14), a tentmaker out of Paul (Acts 18:1-3) and a carpenter out of Jesus (Mark 6:3). The effort to survive is sacred, for without it the human family would perish. Consequently, the good sense that makes up the art of survival has kept mankind sowing and reaping through the ages.

3. Further, financial success is the fulfillment of a divinely given duty. It is every man's earthly responsibility to provide for his family and himself. The Scriptures make nothing plainer than this:

> But if any provide not for his own, and specially for those of his own house, he hath denied the faith, and is worse than an infidel.
>
> I Timothy 5:8

That's God brief on material duty. Very stern! But very right! So there is something worse than infidelity — financial irresponsibility. This topic is a part of religion. It does pertain to the faith. The God of all justice will not join hands with the freeloader. He rather says:

> If any would not work, neither should he eat.
>
> II Thessalonians 3:10

God never meant for able-bodied people to live off the

labors of others, except for brief periods of unusual circumstances. Rather, His economic rule is: *No work, no eat.* An application of this Scripture would reduce the unemployment figure in a hurry.

In the light of the two above Scriptures, it is obvious that a praying tongue and irresponsible hands look a little ridiculous on the same human form. A true view of God never blinds a person to his obligation to care for his family.

Of course, after making provision for today's need and tomorrow's old age, it is self-evident that the making of more money for no worthwhile purpose is no objective blessing and consequently no real success. Yet there is more to be said: The person who makes and saves more wealth than he uses can leave some to his children (if he thinks it will help them) and certainly to good causes; and that, too, is financial success.

The Bible does recognize the right of inheritance, and so does mankind. Understandably, children should assist needy parents, but the more general principle is: "The children ought not to lay up for the parents, but the parents for the children" (II Corinthians 12:15).

4. Monetary competence also means you are on the plus side of sowing and reaping. You sowed and you reaped. Now the gratifying feeling of achievement is yours. Your disciplinary positiveness paid off. The old "I can" spirit of optimism kept you at it; and your optimistic spirit increased with each success.

5. Additionally, a nest egg means freedom from some of the apprehensions that press down on countless numbers throughout the world. There is no fear of the

wolf at the door. Your pantry is full, and as it is consumed you have the funds to replace it.

Neither is there a problem with debts. With no dread of bill collectors, life takes on a freer meaning. No person can hardly call himself free, if he is so shackled with debts that not one dime nor one moment is his. It is as Solomon said, "The borrower is servant to the lender" (Proverbs 22:7). You are not yours if you are over-mortgaged.

Certainly, it is a joy to live in harmony with the Biblical command:

> Owe no man anything.
>
> Romans 13:8

There is no obligation to pay a debt, however, until it is due; if a person is granted 30 or 60 days, he is not in violation of this command as long as he pays in the allotted time. To never pay, even though one did not intend to get himself in an insolvent fix, means that he has still taken what belongs to another, and that might be a veiled form of unintentional theft. "Thou shalt not steal" (Exodus 20:15) is a necessary rule of society. Yes, God can forgive the debtor, but his creditor cannot live on it.

6. Also, financial independence is the fruit of courage and perseverance. It is attained in spite of opposition. Like the kite, the person of self-made wealth has risen against the wind — not with it. Oh, how a little resistance can lift the resolute person. Yes, success is valiant, dauntless and at times almost lionhearted. It's positive, possesses a forward drive. It's energetic, knows the sweat of honest toil. It's persevering, refuses to quit.

No quitter ever goes far.

Prosperity doesn't pick the easiest road but the one that's going to the right place. The prosperous person prefers the road that leads to where he wishes to go instead of the one with the fewest bumps. The man of means — Oh! he has been bumped. But so has the man of no means who chose what he thought was the easy road — Oh! how he has been battered and bruised from a lot of jolts that were not foreseen in the beginning.

So at least some bumps, even for the successful, are down the road. Nevertheless, if you can suffer misfortunes and still go forward, your chances of success ahead are very bright. On the other hand, "no man, having put his hand to the plow, and looking back, is fit for the kingdom of God" (Luke 9:62) — nor is he fit for success in the field of finance.

During the Great Depression a large number of businesses, including many banks, went bankrupt. The fall of each had a domino effect on others. Suicides were common. Many once-rich-but-suddenly-broke people did not know which way to jump, except out of tall buildings and off high bridges. However, I knew one bank president who made a better jump — he jumped to a new life, though he had to start at the lowest level. Penniless, he began to sell old clothing, carrying it in his hands, going on foot from house to house. After a while he was able to rent an old store building and put in a used clothing and furniture business. There his prosperity began to accelerate. He later went into the oil business and became wealthy again. It is hard to keep that kind of man down. The world can flatten him; but, hurting all over, he gets back up again.

Trust in God, self and our free enterprise system can get a person going again. It lets him see that the world is still out there with all its blessings. Of course it takes determination, but behind every self-made fortune, whether large or small, there is spirit and resoluteness. Hence, financial success is definitely related to what the world calls *backbone.*

7. Furthermore, in a complete analysis of material wealth we must recognize that it is something often envied by those who do not attain it. Unfortunate but true. Envy is a terribly rotten thing — "Envy the rottenness of the bones" (Proverbs 14:30). But it is better to be envied and to "suffer for well doing, than for evildoing" (I Peter 3:17). It is preferable to be financially successful and the target of envy and covetousness than to be broke and the object of charity. So go ahead and prosper.

8. Prospering means getting ahead in spite of criticism. Nevertheless, we should be governed by the truth that self-support is a personal trust that goes with the privilege of living here on earth and that no person should be condemned for conscientiously and energetically using thought, time and toil to measure up to it. However, there are always envious people with the grasshopper philosophy who are ready to take a lick at you — if not at your face, at your back — for rising above them. In a futile effort to justify their unprosperous state, they are very profuse in their ugly remarks: "Old money bags." "That skin flint." "Old tightwad." "What's he trying to do, kill himself working?" "I guess he thinks he can take it with him."

But when the little-work-and-lots-of-play, spend-all-and-save-none advocates get in trouble, where do they go? Not to their own kind. You know where they run — to the very people they've chided and tongue lashed. Do not let what they say deter you. For if you have a little nest egg, you can later return good for evil by helping them. And believe me, they'll need it.

9. Another thing we must note is that wealth helps many besides its possessor. It allows the non-possessors to have a lot of things they could not have otherwise. Just think. Our people could not have automobiles, gasoline, refrigerators, air-conditioning, television, prepared foods, cheaper and finer clothing, and even writing paper along with countless other things they daily accept, if it were not for the savings of many hard working, thrifty people. Their accumulations went into the formation of companies that produce goods and services. A company is not a non-human entity but an association of persons banded together for a joint purpose. For instance, there can be a company of people on a fishing trip, a company of persons on a Sunday School picnic, and a company of people in a business venture. A company is human beings. In the case of a business company, it is a band of investors who furnished the capital to make the business a reality, which would have been impossible without finances. And the larger companies have thousands and thousands and even hundreds of thousands of stockholders. Many of them are little investors. But their savings, whether large or small, have made a better life for a world of people. It is as simple as this: no savings, no wealth; no wealth, no investments; no investments, no companies; no companies, no goods as we have today, for the ability to produce would be lacking; and, also, no companies, no place for many people to work.

Here is something else: without the financial success of others, many people could not have an automobile, home or furniture because they obtain them on credit. You say, "But they got the financing from the bank or the savings and loan company." Yes, but where did the bank and the loan company get the money? Neither used a printing press to run off that money. It came from people who have had a certain degree of financial success.

As an example: A young couple buys a home with money lent to them from a savings and loan company, which got the money from an elderly couple living in the same block. So indirectly, the young couple got the money for their house from their neighbors. That is the way our economy works. Without the financial success of some people, we never would have reached our present material standards. Everybody profits from the saver. Yes, our whole society shares to some extent in the blessings of wealth, and without it we would still be in the primitive state; so it hardly behooves any to be unappreciative of those who make such possible.

10. Furthermore, financial prosperity means you can give larger amounts to religion, the government and other causes. And this is success!

Unquestionably, in the eyes of God, the widow's two mites are very acceptable — that is for her (Mark 12:41-44); nevertheless, one look at church budgets will convince you that the mites will not finance the work the churches plan. The more one makes and has, the more he can and should give in dollars and cents (I Corinthians 16:2); and thus with sizable earnings and proportionate giving, bigger budgets can be met. Visualize the program of the church, if it received nothing but mites; it still could do many good works, but the expensive items would be prohibitive: large and commodious buildings, parking lots, paid staff, paid missionaries, radio and television time, et cetera.

Also, the prosperous person contributes more financially to the economic structure of our government; for you pay taxes on your profits — the more profits, the more taxes, even at an increasing rate. Think what would happen to our government, to Social Security and to all other Federal services, if there were no prosperous people. One thing our government ought to encourage — if for no other reason, at least for the sake of itself — is personal and corporate prosperity. For without money, the government would fail.

Civil government has to be supported by the people, and it is a part of religion that we do it. For "the powers that be are ordained by God" (Romans 13:1). Jesus said, "Render therefore unto Caesar the things which are Caesar's; and unto God the things that are God's" (Matthew 22:21). Hence, the government should respect the conscience of religion, and religion should support the government. And one of the ways to support government is the payment of taxes. Jesus did (Matthew 17:24-27). This necessitates prosperity.

THINK ON THESE THINGS

1. Is the right of inheritance Biblical?
2. To whom do the needy go when they are in trouble?
3. What is the relationship between man and "bread"?
4. What is worse than being an infidel?
5. In God's plan, what is the relationship between working and eating?
6. Why do some criticize the prosperous people? Is such criticism ever justified?
7. How does wealth bless even those who do not possess great wealth?
8. How would church work and church budgets be changed if some of the members were not financially prosperous?

THREE

Our Birthright — The Right to Prosper

MAN'S BEING IN the image of God befits a proud birth, a life of rulership on the earth and a life of plenty:

> And God said, Let us make man in our image, after our likeness; and let them have dominion over the fish of the sea, and over the fowl of the air, and over the cattle, and over all the earth, and over every creeping thing that creepeth upon the earth.
>
> Genesis 1:26

MAN'S INNATE RIGHT

1. This is the fitting birthright that was given to man in that early day by his Creator:

> And God blessed them, and God said unto them, Be fruitful, and multiply, and replenish the earth, and subdue it: and have dominion over the fish of the sea, and over the fowl of the air, and over every living thing that moveth upon the earth.
>
> And God said, Behold, I have given you every herb bearing seed, which is upon the face of all the earth, and every tree, in the which is the fruit of a tree yielding seed; to you it shall be for meat.
>
> And to every beast of the earth, and to every fowl of the air, and to every thing that creepeth upon the earth, wherein there is life, I have given every green herb for meat: and it was so.

> And God saw everything that he had made, and behold,
> it was very good.
>
> Genesis 1:28-31

Therein is man's charter for the possession of the earth. That is God's commission for man to utilize for his necessities, comfort and enjoyment the immense resources of the earth, by agricultural productions, mining operations, scientific discoveries, mechanical inventions and manufacturing aids. The whole earth with all its boundless opportunities is the heritage of man. His noble and dignified state — a creature in the image of God — enforces his right to use the earth and to be blessed by it. Indeed *man was meant to prosper!*

And all of this, as the Scripture states, is something God looked upon as being *good.* And what God calls *good,* man should not call *bad.* Of course, any good thing can be perverted and misused, but this does not indict the constitutional goodness of it.

2. In a further elaboration of man's birthright to material success and the enjoyment of it, Solomon stated:

> Behold that which I have seen: it is good and comely
> for one to eat and to drink, and to enjoy the good of all
> his labor that he taketh under the sun all the days of his
> life, which God giveth him: for it is his portion.
>
> Every man also to whom God hath given riches and
> wealth, and hath given him power to eat thereof, and to
> take his portion, and to rejoice in his labor; this is the gift
> of God.
>
> Ecclesiastes 5:18,19

We see two important lessons in the passage: (1) The private incentive system. (2) What is called a *portion* —

"riches and wealth" — is a gift of God. And God does not give that which is within itself evil. To the contrary, material blessings are described as good and perfect (James 1:17).

3. Yes, it is most certainly true that "a man's life consisteth not in the abundance of the things which he possesseth" (Luke 12:15). Nevertheless, the text acknowledges that life does consist in things but not in the *abundance* of things. This is very evident. For a person can eat only one mouthful at a time, wear only one suit at a time and occupy only one room at a time. Life which is lived momentarily requires only a limited amount each moment. But this does not argue that it is improper for a person to have a storehouse of food, other suits and other rooms. The passage was given to rebuke greed and covetousness — not to condemn plenty. The abundance of things does not add to the most satisfying living, which goes deeper than materials. But the fact that there is a spiritual part of man which has needs that materials will not fill does not lessen his physical requirements. So we must recognize that the abundance of things can support man's necessary, physical needs in bad weather, illness, misfortune and old age, though it can be used only momentarily and must be left behind when he leaves. While life does not *consist* in the abundance of things, it does *concern* things.

So this innate right to financial success makes for a joyful birth. *Man is born to have.* It is his birthright. God placed you with all your abilities and potentials on this earth with all its benefits and opportunities. As you look across the earth, the command of God rings in your ears, "Subdue it."

THE POTENTIAL FOR PROSPEROUS LIVING

Man the best of God's creation should not be expected to live on the worst. To do so, contradicts the design of all the earth.

1. The potential to eat well is before us. The Creator has given us many sources of food, but we have to sweat to get them — "in the sweat of thy face shalt thou eat bread" (Genesis 3:19). The never-sweats do not like this, but it is rebellion toward a law of Him who made them. You cannot live well by just licking a knife. Anybody knows that it is good to have a purse and a palate that match.

The trees are here for lumber, the clay for bricks and the iron ore for steel. Hence, if a person wants a larger house than some have, then let him sweat a little more (the basic law of having) — let him cut down a few more trees, make a few more bricks, do a little more mining and work a little harder to put it together.

The energy sources are here and all man has to do to go faster than the horse, to stay warmer than the wintry blast, and to stay cooler than the summer sun, is to use them. To contend that it is wrong to harness these powers to the good of our earthly sojourn contradicts the handiwork of God. But our having these material benefits puts us in a category that is called *financial success.*

2. Since material prosperity requires the sweat that is spoken of in Genesis 3:19, the question arises, *Is the reward worth the effort?* For there is one thing sure, material achievement does not come free — free of planning, free of effort, free of thrift, free of discipline. So

the question always pops up, *Is it worth it?* The person who prefers to sleep under the shade tree does not think so, and for this reason he will never have a place in the sun.

For the law of effort is unyielding.

> God reaches us good things by our own hands.
> God gives the milk but not the bucket.
> Self do, self have.
> God helps them that help themselves.

So you do not have to be born with a silver spoon in your mouth to have one. The God who created you also created the silver in the ground. Now it is up to you. The Lord has given power to get wealth (Deuteronomy 8:18). Since God put the material blessings out there and gave man the power to obtain them, surely He meant for man to avail himself of them. Assuredly, the Creator meant for man between birth and death to have something better than a mere existence.

OUR FOREFATHERS

Our God-fearing, rugged ancestors believed in this land of opportunity —

> *Where ask is have, where seek is find,*
> *Where knock is open wide.*
>
> *Christopher Smart*

Consequently, they blazed trails, cleared forests, raised cities and left eloquent words in historic documents that should swell our hearts with inspiration and move our hands to perspiration. Two centuries later, it is highly appropriate that we call attention to one of those expressive papers:

> *That all men are by nature equally free and indepen-*
> *dent, and have certain inherent rights, of which, when they*
> *enter into a state of society, they cannot by any compact*
> *deprive or divest their posterity; namely, the enjoyment of*
> *life and liberty, with the means of acquiring and possess-*
> *ing property, and pursuing and obtaining happiness and*
> *safety.*
>
> George Mason
> Virginia Bill of Rights
> [June 12, 1776], Art. 1

Born for success — our pioneer parents believed this is an inalienable right, that the God who gave us life, gave us a world to occupy and the right to reap its benefits at the same time. This is the birthright to which the Creator and His laws of nature entitle each individual.

The right to succeed in a land of opportunity — our forefathers called it *The American Dream.* Many waked up to make it a reality. They believed there was plenty in a smiling land, and they read their fate in their own vision. Indeed, they had their share of troubles. But they had no sense of ills to come that could not be met, for they knew the world would keep on turning and that only a part of everyday would be darkness.

Struggles — that is what life is made of, but a full stomach makes many of them easier to bear.

POVERTY

Ever since man was driven out of the Garden of Eden, *one of humanity's common battles is against a common enemy — poverty;* and where it has not been conquered, life has been hard. While the *"love* of money [not money, the *love* of it] is the root of all evil" (I Timothy 6:10), the *lack* of money is the root of many woes. Sure, poverty is better than some things — greed, dishonesty, etc. — but it is no blessed estate.

Henry Ward Beecher put it this way: "Poverty is very good in poems but very bad in the house, very good in maxims and sermons but very bad in practical life." Impoverishment is sometimes praised by those who have never really borne it long, for it is easier to praise than to bear. Thus, in practicality we are forced to say that destitution is a source of much distress in the world.

Poverty is a prolific breeding ground of crime, because the devil can also dance well in an empty pocket. Indeed, it is a source of the ugliest misdeeds and the blackest evils. It tempts persons to consent to things they would not otherwise do.

> *My poverty, but not my will consents*
> *William Shakespeare*

Unquestionably, poverty is no safeguard to morals. To the contrary, it is a nagging enticement to wrongdoing. Yes, an empty stomach is hard to cope with, so difficult that it was used as one of the temptations of Jesus (Matthew 4:1-4). He overcame, but weaker ones bow.

It was the wise old Benjamin Franklin who said: "Poverty often deprives a man of all spirit and virtue; it is hard for an empty bag to stand upright."

And the pertinent comment of the brilliant Voltaire is painfully true the world over: "The poor man is never free; he serves in every country."

> *Oh! poverty is a weary thing, 'tis full of*
> *grief and pain.*

> *It keepeth down the joys of man, as*
> *with an iron chain;*
> *It maketh even the little child with*
> *heavy signs complain.*
>
> *Mary Hawitt*

So — "the association of poverty with progress is the great enigma of our times," states Henry George.

WEALTHY MEN AND WOMEN OF GOD

It is interesting therefore to note that *many of the illustrious characters of the Bible* — distinguished men and women of God, great in faith, dedication and service — *were also well-off materially.*

— Abraham: "And Abram was very rich in cattle, in silver, and in gold" (Genesis 13:2).

— Lot: "And Lot also, which went with Abraham, had flocks, and herds, and tents. And the land was not able to bear them, that they might dwell together: for their substance was great" (Genesis 13:5,6).

— Isaac: "Then Isaac sowed in that land, and received in the same year a hundred-fold: and the Lord blessed him. And the man waxed great, and went forward, and grew until he became very great: For he had possessions of flocks, and possessions of herds" (Genesis 26:12-14).

— Jacob: "And I have oxen, and asses, flocks and manservants, and womenservants" (Genesis 32:5).

— Joseph: Concerning his financial ability to aid his famine-stricken father and brothers we read, "And there will I nourish thee; for yet there are five years of famine; lest thou, and thy household, and all thou hast, come to poverty" (Genesis 45:11).

— Boaz: "A mighty man of wealth" (Ruth 2:1).

— Jehoshaphat: "And he had riches and honor in abundance" (II Chronicles 17:5).

— Hezekiah: "Had exceeding much riches and honor . . . for God had given him substance very much" (II Chronicles 32:27-29).

— Job: "His substance also was seven thousand sheep, and three thousand camels, and five hundred yoke of oxen, and five hundred she asses, and a very great household; so that this man was the greatest of all the men of the east" (Job 1:3).

— Joseph of Arimathea: "A rich man of Arimathea, named Joseph, who also himself was Jesus' disciple: He went to Pilate, and begged the body of Jesus . . .wrapped it in a clean linen cloth, and laid it in his own new tomb" (Matthew 27:57-60). It is significant that when public opinion turned against Jesus and He was executed, that when other disciples feared and ran, the one who had enough courage and heart to give Jesus a considerate and beautiful burial was a rich man.

— Zaccheus: "And he was rich" (Luke 19:2). It is meaningful to observe that his riches did not keep salvation from coming to him (verse 9).

— Lydia: "A seller of purple" (Acts 16:14). It is noteworthy that her business did not interfere with her hearing and obeying the word of the Lord.

CONCLUSION

Yes, it is evident, "we brought nothing into this

world, and it is certain we can carry nothing out" (I Timothy 6:7); but between our entrance into the world and our exit from it materials are an absolute necessity. And, as our birthright, God placed them here for us to gather and to use — not for vainglory but for our good.

> *Wealth to us is not mere material for vainglory but an opportunity for achievement; and poverty we think is no disgrace to acknowledge but a real degradation to make no effort to overcome.*
>
> *Thucydides*
> *460-400 B.C.*

And now in deep reflection, we recall the most foolhardy business deal of all times, Esau's selling his birthright to his brother Jacob for "bread and pottage of lentils" (Genesis 25:33,34). Relevantly, many today sell their God-given birthright to material success for another dish — a dish of indolence, waste and thoughtlessness. The worst poverty is not little bread but little ambition. For this, man must pay a price — and with interest.

THINK ON THESE THINGS

1. Would you agree that *man was meant to prosper?*
2. How did our forefathers feel about acquiring and possessing property?
3. What is your birthright?
4. Is poverty really desirable? Or is poverty better in poetry than in practice? What are the dangers of poverty?

5. Is God's approval of wealth only found in the Old Testament?
6. How is poverty of physical materials a minor problem compared to the poverty of ambition?
7. How are we surrounded by the potential for prosperous living?
8. How are we to interpret the Biblical passage, "Life consisteth not in the abundance of things" with man's need for things?

FOUR

Faith and Mountains

IN THE PRECEDING chapter we noted that financial prosperity is the birthright of man. It is something the Creator wills for him to enjoy. This was explicitly stated by the Apostle John in his brief letter to Gaius: "Beloved, I wish above all things that thou mayest prosper and be in health, even as thy soul prospereth" (III John 2). That is how long and to what extent a person can prosper materially and still be blessed by it: just as long as his soul prospers. Just that long — whether little or much — it is helpful.

"I wish . . . that thou mayest prosper," stated the Apostle John.

1. But for it to come to pass, *a person must believe that he can.* There are still plenty of opportunities to succeed for the people who believe they can. It is the "I can'ters" who have to live on the crumbs, while the "I caners" get the bigger portions. The doubters are doomed to failure; they lose the reward that others win.

> *I find no foeman in the road but Fear.*
> *To doubt is failure and to dare Success.*
> *Frederic Lawrence Knowles*

> *Our doubts are traitors,*
> *And make us lose the good we oft might win,*
> *By fearing to attempt.*
> *William Shakespeare*

2. Truly, the Biblical definition of faith also fits well one's belief in material reaping: "the substance of things hoped for, the evidence of things not seen" (Hebrews 11:1). Indeed, this is the nature of all true faith. Faith gives substance or confidence to the things hoped for; it is the basis, ground and support of it, though at the time it is not seen. It gives the force of reality to that which is believed and influences us as if we actually saw the desired object. The belief that a certain undertaking will be profitable leads men to go into it. Faith wields a powerful influence over the lives and fortunes of those who possess it. The farmer sows in faith; he believes the harvest will be forthcoming and acts as if it were already achieved.

As mentioned in the previous chapter, Isaac sowed and reaped a hundred-fold (Genesis 26:12-14). His belief that he could prosper paid off. For each grain he planted, he harvested a hundred. He was not stopped by the doubts that come from thinking on the possibility of hot winds that scorch the sprouting or severe clouds that destroy the harvest.

> He that observeth the wind shall not sow; and he that regardeth the clouds shall not reap.
>
> Ecclesiastes 11:4

In doubt and despair, he could have eaten the seed corn and all would have been gone; but in saving the seed and planting it, he reaped a hundred times as much.

Don't eat the seed corn. Something saved today may bring you a hundred times as much tomorrow. One thing sure, something must be saved now if you would have more later. But nobody does this unless he believes in the possibility of improving his lot.

3. Yes, it is faith that gives us the energy and tenacity to overcome our problems, both spiritual and material. "And this is the victory that overcometh the world, even our faith" (I John 5:4). With it, we move. "We walk by faith" (II Corinthians 5:7).

Faith moves mountains — all kinds of mountains, including mountains of mediocrity and poverty. Do not confuse faith, however, with wishful thinking. For wishful thinking will not move even an ant hill. You cannot wish yourself into prosperity and leadership. But by believing you can achieve, you can. There is nothing mystical or magical about the moving power of faith. It simply gives you the "positive-I-can" view. It puts you in forward gear and gives you the energy to go. The how-to-get-there then begins to develop.

4. The forceful, successful people are people of faith. You will find faith behind every successful project — church, business, politics and finance. You can be sure the people who have very little faith in themselves and in what they are doing will not make much progress. In fact, I have never seen a doubting success. The doubters always fail. They think they cannot do any better and consequently they do not.

You have heard, "Well, I tried it, but I never did think it would work." It didn't.

Here is a little lesson on psychology: When the mind doubts, it subconsciously comes up with the arguments to support the disbelief. Then the mind just automatically begins to condition itself to failure, not really wanting to succeed. The status quo enjoys certain comfort, while success disturbs a person from his routine of ease.

Not caring to succeed, which begins with doubt, is the cause of most failures.

Believe you can succeed and you will succeed.

Think failure and you will fail.

So the first thing to do in changing from failure to success is to change from doubt to faith. Believe in yourself. Believe you can make it with God's help.

The children of Israel made progress in their journey to the Promised Land of Canaan as long as they believed. It was when their faith turned to doubt that they wanted to return to their Egyptian slavery (Exodus 14:10-12). And today the same thing enslaves: Doubt!

I want to tell you about a couple that helped themselves by overcoming doubt. With just a small salary, they had believed it was impossible to accumulate anything. Consequently, they made no effort. For years they lived more or less from hand to mouth, paying their rent, saving nothing, and trying to console themselves in the thought that there would be more for them in the next world. And it is excellent to anticipate the greatest rewards in the world to come, but *man the best of God's creation should not be expected to live on the worst in this life*. Nevertheless, something finally happened to this couple to give them more faith and courage. They decided they could lay up a nest egg. Believing this, they began to do it. They later bought a home. Still later, they bought some land on his G.I. right to borrow. Today the home is paid for. The land was sold for a big profit. They have a large savings account and are able to live much more comfortably in the senior years which are slipping up on them. Their success began with faith. A working, moving faith is one prerequisite of attainment that cannot be over-stressed.

Another inspiring example comes to mind: Years ago I spent a few days in the home of a family that had come up the hard way to a level of financial comfort and security. They were devout, consecrated Christians. In this elegant, southern city, they lived in a large, white two-story, colonial home that sat on a little hill, draped in pines and greenery, which gave it a beautiful, commanding appearance. They had suffered in the Great Depression as many Americans had. But the man had faith. He had a dream. It began with popcorn and peanuts. It would not take much capital to start a popcorn and peanut business in the city park and zoo. He got the concession and he was in business. There was more profit in it than others had ever dreamed. Later he got other concessions. He prospered. It was faith that started things to popping. It always does. It gives the right mental attitude. So man's main problem is to increase his faith.

HOW TO INCREASE YOUR FAITH

1. Think on the handiwork of God. Surely He would not have created this world with all its blessings and placed man on it for its rulership, if He had not intended for man to have the good things of earth. This is why the first two chapters are devoted to this matter. It is basic. It enhances faith. God wants you to succeed — if you can bear success. So why should you doubt? Why be afraid?

Jesus used the example of God's feeding the little birds to increase the faith of doubters, with the assuring thought that man is much better than birds (Matthew 6:25-26). Yes, the little birds have to work — a universal law of God — but the point is *the provisions are here for the taking.* So it is with man; his needs have been provided by his Maker. All he has to do is to believe this and go to work, which is much better than a life of worry and anxiety. Be not anxious. Believe!

> *God's in his heaven.*
> *All's right with the world*
> *Robert Browning*

"I have been young, and now am old; yet have I not seen the righteous forsaken, nor his seed begging bread," declared the Psalmist (Psalms 37:25).

2. Think success. Every person eventually becomes what he thinks. "For as he thinketh in his heart, so is he" (Proverbs 23:7). Wherever you are, at home or at work or at play, think about succeeding — not failing. When facing a problem, think, "I will conquer, I will win." When opportunity comes, think, "I can handle it." Let your dominating thought be, "I will succeed." Thinking success starts your mind to figuring out how to reach it. Nobody wins them all, but with this attitude you will have a winning streak.

3. Read success. As one reads, he thinks; and as he thinks, he is. This is one of the reasons for this volume. We can change the world with books. Why go to the trouble to learn to read, if you never do it to your advantage?

4. Associate with positive, I-can-do-it people. For the pessimism of the I-can'ters may rub off on you. The fearful status-quoers have at times hurt a lot of us. "Better

leave well enough alone," they told us. I am glad the people who financed Columbus did not listen. The status-quoers never discover a new world; they are afraid to get out of their old one.

CONCLUSION

Success depends on attitude, and nothing gives you a more winning outlook than faith. Hence, the First Step is: *believe you can succeed.* Then the aims will develop.

THINK ON THESE THINGS

1. What did the Apostle John wish for Gaius?
2. Why does the definition of faith fit well one's belief in material reaping?
3. Do you believe that attitudes make a difference? Do you really believe you can be more financially prosperous?
4. What is the seed corn of your financial future? Have you been *eating* it or *planting* it?
5. What is the difference between faith and wishful thinking?
6. What status quo financial conditions in your life are comfortable? Which ones are uncomfortable enough to make you do something about them?
7. What can you do this week to improve your "success attitude"?
8. What small changes can you make in your vocabulary and daily habits that will increase your success attitudes?

Set Your Sails

BEFORE DOING ANYTHING there must be the aiming or purposing of it. This is God's way:

> I have purposed it, I will also do it.
>
> Isaiah 46:11

1. The way to get things done is to set goals.

Your ship will not come in unless you send it out. Complacency will sink it. But aiming your ship at distant ports will send it out that it may return richly laden. "Oh, if only my ship would come in," moans the wishful thinker. But it will not for he has not sent it out. He has not set his sails for success.

The reason some people never hit anything is they never aim.

> *In the long run men hit only what they aim at.*
>
> *Henry David Thoreau*

The big majority of all families have no specific aims to attain financial strength. This is why they have no definite plans, for there can be no plans where there are no goals. Inasmuch as success depends upon organized effort, then it is easy to see why that all success is predicated on aims or purposes. Without an aim, man is like a piece of driftwood floating down the stream of ease. That is easier until he hits the rocks and rapids.

2. The only thing some people do to get ahead is to pass the buck to Jehovah God. They passively say, "Trust God." Do not misunderstand me, please, for trust in God is smart and commendable — more is needed. But the truth is, they do not trust Him, not enough to do what He says. They need to learn that faith without works is dead (James 2:17). In their case, their words are only a futile effort to justify a grasshopper philosophy of living in which there is little effort, much spending, no thrift and no discipline. Their spirit is so different from the spirit of Him who said: "In the sweat of thy face shalt thou eat bread" (Genesis 3:19). "He that tilleth his land shall have plenty of bread: but he that followeth after vain persons shall have poverty; enough" (Proverbs 28:19). "Gather up the fragments that remain, that nothing be lost" (John 6:12).

There just has to be something wrong with a philosophy that scorns financial responsibility and abuses successful people. For in the long run, individual success is the basis of every society. Yet much of today's political rhetoric appeals to, glorifies and favors the shiftless spendthrift. This has given rise to a rapidly developing national insolvency that necessitates that all government inks turn red and flow as if there is no tomorrow. But when today's spending is over, tomorrow's interest payments shall have only begun. It is so glaringly contradictory for people who profess such an aversion to riches to always have their hands stuck out. I hope you remember. I hope America remembers.

The person with no material goals is sure to be a victim of the world's economic treadmill — no progress. *Without goals we cannot go.*

3. Knowing where he is going — aims — is a distinctive trait of man. One thing that distinguishes man from the beast is what he may have and his aim to get it. Hence, man is not the total of what he has, but the aggregate of what he does not have that he might have. Man — how great are his possibilities!

4. Goals are not just dreams. They are human hopes that are clear and categorical, practical and powerful. And as a person acts upon his goals, his goals act upon him. They are absolutely necessary to success.

Any up-and-going business sets goals ten and fifteen years ahead. This adds *motivation and direction* to their efforts. Making up your mind what you want for yourself and your family ten years from now is highly motivating.

When once you have set a goal, in the same process you *tap an extra supply of energy* to reach it. Psychology tells us that people with goals do not tire as easily as drifters with no goals.

Also, there is *coordinating and unifying power* in an objective. It keeps you from going off after yonder calls. It is thought that Noah did a better job of living while he was fulfilling his aim — building an ark. It was when it was all over, with no unifying goal, that he went to pieces (Genesis 9:20,21).

Reaching your objective is not as strenuous as it may at first appear. It is only a step-by-step program. In the beginning it may seem like a long way off; but it is not far to the next step, and that is the way you reach it. And when you look at the whole of life, there is one thing sure: it is an encouragement to take that step.

John Ruskin said: "There is only one way of seeing things rightly, and that is seeing the whole of them."

5. The aimless person can always find an excuse for his failure or mediocrity. However, Solomon was not fooled. He was wise to the unambitious person's vain efforts to rationalize his indolence, and thus gave us this ever-relevant Scripture:

> The slothful man saith, There is a lion without, I shall
> be slain in the streets.
>
> Proverbs 22:13

But what some think are ferocious lions are only friendly kittens.

Lion or no lion, one of the attributes of all successful people is their courage to overcome difficulties. The rain does not stop them; they get raincoats. Neither do the hills; they just push down a little more on the accelerator. Nor do the rivers; they build bridges. Things will always come up to upset your plans. Nevertheless, the successful people — devoted to their aims — face their problems and triumph.

But poor Joe has never learned this. He just goes around saying, "I've never had any good luck." And he hasn't. The reason: he never aimed to be successful.

> *You will find that luck*
> *Is only pluck*
> *To try things over and over;*
> *Patience and skill,*
> *Courage and will,*
> *Are the four leaves of luck's clover.*

So do not wait for fortune to come. Go out and seek it.

> *Do not, then, sit idly waiting*
> *For some greater work to do;*
> *Fortune is a lazy goddess —*
> *She will never come to you.*
>
> *G.M. Grannis*

Poor Joe. He thinks all the opportunities are gone; but there are still plenty of them, more than most of us are willing to seize. Remember — the best of everything has not yet been realized.

6. If you want something good to happen to you, aim at it. I have heard several say, "I wish I could strike an oil well." My reply was, "Do you have any oil royalty?" "No." "Do you have any oil leases?" "No." And I would continue, "Then in your present state there is no way you can strike oil. But if you really want oil, go where a well has been brought in and try to learn its developing trend and then buy a lease or some royalty out in that direction."

It is amazing what you can do when you plan.

Years ago I walked over a man's farm, marvelling at its fertility, thriving crops, thoroughbred cattle, adequate barns and commodious house. It was all paid for, the fruit of a disciplined life. The owner's brief comment was, "I did it on purpose."

Concerning commodious living, we read from the Scriptures:

> And because the haven was not commodious to winter in, the more part advised to depart thence also, if by any means they might attain to Phenice, and there to winter.
>
> Acts 27:12

Also, Titus 3:12.

In the late fall of last year I visited on the warm Padre Island in the Gulf of Mexico off the Texas coast. One thing I noticed: Several retired citizens were there for the winter to escape the frozen season of the North. It takes money to do this ("money is a defense," Ecclesiastes 7:12), which means they had it. They would not have had it, however, if plans had not been previously made and executed. In years gone by they had worked for savings, so it was only right that their savings now work for them.

For the sake of emphasis, I repeat: *having requires aiming.*

I know a lady who clearly demonstrated this. She and her husband were tenant farmers that moved every year or two. Life was hard. It took all they made just to live. But one day the good wife resolved to change their state. She told her husband to pursue his farming as he had, that she would help him as much as she could, but that she was going into business for herself. She had decided to put in a little sweet potato plant farm. She, with her own hands, put out the potato beds, cared for the plants, advertised in a farm magazine and the orders started coming. In a short time she made enough to buy a farm. As more profits were earned she bought a larger farm. A helpful wife — a help mate for her husband, Genesis 2:18 — can add much to the economic structure of a family. Solomon describes her as a worthy woman (Proverbs 31:10-31). More is said about her in Chapter XII. A person can really be successful when he or she is properly motivated. Too many, however, are not impelled; they are only wishful thinkers.

Now, *the more important thing is not where you are but where you want to go.* You can go and you can arrive by aiming.

7. So let each of us aim:

1) To be self-supporting: to earn his own bread (Genesis 3:19), to carry his own weight — not to expect something for nothing. Remember — nobody owes you anything for having been born.

2) To care for his own (I Timothy 5:8), to give them the advantages nature has to offer.

3) To have the resources to live in keeping with the dignity that should characterize a creature made in the image of God (Genesis 1:27).

4) To have a commodious, livable home that he can enjoy and in which he can entertain (Luke 10:38).

5) To have the funds to care for and to educate his children (Proverbs 22:6).

6) To have the financial strength that exempts him from worry over bills that come due (Romans 13:8).

7) To be able to take vacations and see the wonders of God, to recharge himself physically, mentally and spiritually. At times all of us need a rest (Psalms 55:6,7).

8) To have a surplus of assets that will allow him to ride out the bad days without strain and tension (Proverbs 6:6-8).

9) To have a balance that gives comfort, plenty and security in old age rather than have only a skimpy existence.

10) To have some wealth to give his children that they may get off to a faster start (II Corinthians 12:14).

For all of this to be realized, one must follow the Biblical principle that there is a time and a season to get: just as there is a time to put the roof on — before it starts raining; and a time to sow — before you plan to harvest.

> To everything there is a season, and a time to every purpose under the heaven ... a time to get.
>
> Ecclesiastes 3:1-6

"A time to get" — that time is NOW while you have strength and opportunity. So, Step Number Two is: *aim to get.*

THINK ON THESE THINGS

1. Why is it wrong to abuse hardworking, thrifty people?
2. Which is more important, where you are or where you want to go?
3. Does "trusting God" mean we have no specific financial goals?
4. How are your goals and your God related?
5. Even if you never reach all of your goals, what are some of the advantages of *having* goals?
6. Write down all the "lions in the street," the excuses for your current situation. Are any of them *really* a limitation? Now throw the list away and ask God to help you get rid of all your limitations and excuses.

7. Goals are not just wishes or dreams. What are your *realistic* financial goals for each of the next five years?
8. Now be more specific about your goals. State them very clearly and specifically. What can you do this week to begin achieving them?

That You May Have

As MENTIONED IN the preceding chapter, it is essential that we have a goal, but that does not bring us to it. Doing something does.

1. God's plan to get is to get with it — work. This is His uniform and immutable requirement for man to obtain material benefits:

> Let him labor ... that he may have.
>
> Ephesians 4:28

It is as Henry Ford said: "There will never be a system invented which will do away with the necessity of work."

2. Every handiwork of God bears the impress of the law of labor. The earth, the air and the water teem with laborious life. Life of every sort is busy working out the problem of its own existence. Nature never quits. Age after age it unceasingly pursues its course which is a perpetual lesson on industry to man. The song of labor rings out from earth's thousand voices, saying WORK. And wise is the person who listens.

> *All nature seems at work. Slugs leave their lair —*
> *The bees are stirring — birds are on the wing —*
> *And Winter, slumbering in the open air,*
> *Wears on her smiling face a dream of Spring!*
>
> *Samuel Taylor Coleridge*

Therefore, let us not accuse nature, she is doing her job. Now it is our turn.

3. The very tenor of the Bible is that of work and industry. It is a workaday world we see in the Bible — not an idlers' circus. It begins by telling us of God's work: "And on the seventh day God ended his work which he had made; and he rested on the seventh day from all his work which he had made"(Genesis 2:2). It is significant and exemplary that He worked six days and rested one — not that He worked one and rested six. Also, Jesus knew the sweaty brow that comes from honest and honorable toil. He was a carpenter. He Himself said:

> My Father worketh even until now, and I work.
>
> John 5:17

So, to work is Godlike. Also, the apostles were workingmen. While the Bible speaks of kings and queens, most of the characters are men who tend sheep, plow fields, draw nets, build houses and make tents, and women who keep households, work in fields and sell merchandise.

In the early dawn of time *the Creator made the appointment for man to work:*

> In the sweat of thy face shalt thou eat bread.
>
> Genesis 3:19

And God predicated good times on labor:

> For thou shalt eat the labor of thine hands: happy shalt thou be, and it shall be well with thee.
>
> Psalms 128:2

The passage states three blessings of labor: (1) to have

to eat, (2) to be happy, and (3) to have things well with you.

The law of increase demands labor:

> He that gathereth by labor shall increase.
>
> Proverbs 13:11

It is work rather than talk that is profitable. All talk and no work accomplishes nothing. Just working your lips will not get the job done. In all the rules of success compiled by the people in every age and in every land work has been included. There is no formula for success that will work unless you do. However, a little elbow grease can really make you shine.

> In all labor there is profit: but the talk of the lips tendeth only to penury.
>
> Proverbs 14:23

In a realistic gesture, God *plainly warns of the necessary destitution and want of the sluggard;* and call it what you will, it is a fact of life:

> How long wilt thou sleep, O sluggard? When wilt thou arise out of thy sleep? Yet a little sleep, a little slumber, a little folding of the hands to sleep: So shall thy poverty come as one that traveleth, and thy want as an armed man.
>
> Proverbs 6:9-11

> Slothfulness casteth into a deep sleep; and an idle soul shall suffer hunger.
>
> Proverbs 19:15

> The soul of the sluggard desireth, and hath nothing: but the soul of the diligent shall be made fat.
>
> Proverbs 13:4

"In this life we get nothing save by effort," is Theodore Roosevelt's correct analysis of man's fate. Labor is man's great means of obtaining; without it he can achieve nothing, he can have nothing. Yet some wish to bum their way through life.

The story is told of a tramp who stopped at a farmhouse and asked for food. The farm woman, however, had read in the Scriptures "that if any would not work, neither should he eat." Consequently, she showed him to the wood pile and told him to saw wood for half an hour while she cooked him a hot, delicious breakfast. When she went to get him for breakfast, he was gone and this note was left: "You can tell them you saw me, but you didn't see me saw."

You can just about hear him explaining, "I don't mind using the saw, it's the handle I don't like."

Here is a just standard of remuneration:

> The laborer is worthy of his hire.
>
> Luke 10:7

More labor, more hire; less labor, less hire. The profit motive works well. It is only fair that each be allowed to choose his own work style, cognizant of the fact that it will determine his pay. Diligence and hard work are entitled to greater rewards. And hard work is taught in the Bible: "Whatsoever thy hand findeth to do, do it with thy might" (Ecclesiastes 9:10). If you would succeed, you must learn this lesson.

4. The loafers are the losers. No sweat, no sweet. No pains, no gains.

A young man went into a business and applied for a job; however, he really wanted a position instead of a job. The owner, not needing help, said, "Sorry, but I don't have enough work to keep another fellow busy." "Sir," said the applicant, "I'm sure you have. You don't know what a little bit of work it takes to keep me employed." That attitude is too common and is one of the causes of their down-and-out position.

Two men wake up and face another day. Because of their actions, their day is different and so are their rewards. The footprints of one point to the bank, which are made only by workers — and thinkers. But the sporadic and zigzag tracks of the other lead to — you know where — hard times.

Mr. A and Mr. B were driving trucks, delivering meat to restaurants. Both often expressed a desire to put in a hamburger business for himself. Mr. A acted on his desire. He rented a location and began with little more than an active idea, strong desire and inflexible determination. It was his aim to make the world's best hamburger, to have all the ingredients properly proportioned to have a delicious, savory flavor. He knew that an imbalance of ingredients alter the taste just like it does in a cake or pie or any other dish. He knew there could be too much pickle — too sour a taste; too thick buns — looks big but gives only a mouthful of bread; too much mustard — just a mustard sandwich; too little meat — just a meatless hamburger. He was determined to make the best hamburger rather than to make the most profit off each sale. Today he has four stores.

What about Mr. B? He is still delivering meat for the same wholesale meat company. The difference between the two men is Mr. A is an action man while Mr. B is not. Both had the same idea, but Mr. B thought of too many reasons why he should not do it. He made excuses and perhaps will go to his grave making them. Today their incomes are different, but each determined this for himself.

5. Got a good idea? Then get it going. *Rather than wait for fortune to come, go out and seek it.*

> *The tissue of the life to be*
> *We weave with colors all our own,*
> *And in the field of destiny*
> *We reap as we have sown.*
>
> John Greenleaf Whittier

I know a man who opened a cleaning and pressing plant. He began without any customers, and the people did not rush into his business for they were going other places. He had a challenge. And he met it. He knew that the new people were just as apt to trade with him as anybody else, and more so if he called on them. He did and gave them a coupon to get a suit or dress cleaned free. You know where they started trading. Later he hired a lady to do nothing but call on people. His business prospered. A man of action! He succeeded when others were folding up. He pursued fortune and found it.

The world is filled with opportunities, but the handle on every one of them is *work* and there is no way to grab it unless you take hold of the handle.

I saw a man become affluent by starting out to seine minnows. Lake Texoma had just been built and was attracting lots of fishermen. Minnows were in great demand. This man went to the streams and seined them. It was so profitable that he built his own minnow farm of many acres of ponds and began raising them. His becoming well-to-do was no accident. It was the fruit of sound thinking and hard work.

And again I repeat: *An idea is not enough. It takes work! Hard work!*

All self-made people are hard workers. I have never seen a lazy millionaire. The successful person raises his hat to the past, takes off his coat to the present and rolls up his sleeves to the future. So Step Number Three in God's plan for showing us how to live on the plus side is — *work.* It is a rich blessing.

> *This is the gospel of labor — ring it,*
> *ye bells of the kirk —*
> *The Lord of Love came down from above*
> *to live with the men who work.*
> *This is the rose that he planted, here in*
> *the thorn-cursed soil;*
> *Heaven is blest with perfect rest, but*
> *the blessing of earth is toil.*
>
> *Henry van Dyke*

THINK ON THESE THINGS

1. How does the Bible relate labor to having?
2. What is a just standard of remuneration for workers?
3. What are the blessings that come from work?
4. What are the Biblical passages that teach work?
5. Does the quotation, "We reap as we have sown" apply only to working for a living?
6. What attitudes should we teach our children about work?

7. Are your work habits as productive as you can make them? For example, starting one hour earlier each day, you can add nearly a full day to your work week.
8. Work can be an exciting challenge. What can you do to increase the productivity of your working hours?

SEVEN

Gather Up the Fragments

THE GOD WHO made us, knowing the best way for us to live, taught us to be frugal and thrifty. Yet this basic principle of life is presently being scorned. Today there are many who think economy is almost a social crime. This shows how far our society has swung away from the old self-preserving principles set forth by the Creator. But let the jesters roar in their falsity, truth will laugh last. For (1) there is no way to get without getting with it, and (2) no way to keep without saving. It violates Scripture, nature and common sense — all three — to think that we can have by wasting.

THE BIBLE SPEAKS

1. The Bible teaches thrift as a sound principle of economics, and the failure to learn it is called foolish:

> There is treasure to be desired and oil in the dwelling of the wise; but a foolish man spendeth it up.
>
> Proverbs 21:20

The passage distinguishes the wise and the foolish by calling attention to their spending habits. A dollar wasted by a fool is sure to be gained by a wiser person.

2. The Bible speaks of two infamous brothers in the field of finance, the slothful man and the waster.

> He also that is slothful in his work is brother to him
> that is a great waster.
>
> Proverbs 18:9

If money runs through your pocket like water runs through a sieve, then do not be surprised to find that your purse is usually empty.

3. One of the saddest and most pathetic stories in all the Bible is that of the Prodigal Son; however, it has a happy ending for he came to himself (Luke 15:11-32). It is a story of wastefulness: wasted life and wasted substance. After this young man demanded and secured his inheritance, he went "into a far country, and there wasted his substance in riotous living. And when he had spent all, there arose a mighty famine in the land and he began to be in want."

"Willful waste brings woeful want." And in this case, the want was extremely woeful and wretched. He was reduced to the low level of hog pen living and desired even the husks which the swine refused to eat.

Three key, economic thoughts in the story are: (1) "wasted his substance," (2) "when he had spent all," and (3) "began to be in want." It just works that way. Waste and want go together and cannot be separated long. If he had known and heeded what Solomon said, he would have been spared this humiliating ordeal. What did Solomon say? He said this — a principle of economics — which was true yesterday, is true today and shall be true tomorrow:

> He that loveth pleasure shall be a poor man: he that
> loveth wine and oil shall not be rich.
>
> Proverbs 21:17

So godliness can save a person from a way of life that bankrupts both morally and financially.

Because of the circumstances surrounding the Prodigal Son's leaving home, he may have thought his father was a tightwad. But the father became wealthy because he was thrifty, and the son became a pauper because he was wasteful. However, the boy learned in the School of Hard Knocks, but the tuition was awfully high. By the time he got home, ragged and tattered with his stomach pulled in against his backbone, I am sure he was not wanting to give any lectures on finance nor on what he perhaps had once thought was the old man's penny-pinching ways.

Right here we need to recognize that there is a vast difference between frugality and tightwadness. For instance, a saving, frugal person may walk two blocks to save a quarter and when he gets there give $500 to a good cause. You can hardly call that person stingy. Thrifty? Yes. Tightfisted? No.

The Story of the Prodigal Son is recognized as one of the greatest pieces of literature in all the world. There are several major lessons in it; however, in this book we are using only the one on wastefulness. I hope we learn. I hope America learns.

4. Furthermore, it is helpful to recall that another one of the most fascinating and fundamental lessons on finance was taught by Jesus Christ:

> Gather up the fragments that remain that nothing be lost.
>
> John 6:12

This command from Jesus pertaining to materials is undoubtedly shocking to some. But His concern for the people's welfare, both spiritual and physical, caused him to teach thrift and against wastefulness. Thus to waste is wrong, to save is right. After Jesus had multiplied the loaves and fishes and abundantly fed five thousand men, He commanded that the left-overs be collected that nothing be lost. The leavings were twelve baskets full that otherwise would have been wasted. We do not know how big the baskets were; and, in proportion to such a multitude, perhaps the amount saved was not large, but Jesus knew it should be saved. Jesus taught thrift. How many churches are teaching it today?

Now let us recognize and subscribe to the fact that Jesus was not a scabby skinflint. He did not tell them to eat less. It was not a hunger party. To the contrary, "they were filled." So the point He was making is for man *to be economical,* which is a far cry from being miserly, skimpy and abusive of self. May we always make this distinction.

A fool may make money, but it takes a wise person to know how to spend it.

And a dollar saved is twice made.

Yes, it is true, "There won't be any pockets in your shroud"; and it is just as true, unless you fill a pocket, you will not have a shroud unless somebody else pays for it.

THE HABIT OF SAVING

1. Nevertheless, when the subject of saving money comes up, some react, "I can't; there's no way I can." Look out, you are being negative; and, as mentioned in

a previous chapter, you must be positive to succeed. You must think positively, talk positively and act positively. You can. Yes, you can.

How? By forming the habit of saving. Then abundance shall begin to accumulate and multiply. I know this sounds simple but it works. Many simple things are very workable. Habits are simple, yet the Law of Habit goes far in shaping a person's destiny, both spiritually and materially.

> All habits gather by unseen degrees;
> As brooks make rivers, rivers run to seas.
>
> John Dryden

The habit of saving gathers by degrees and makes a brook that makes a river that runs to the Sea of Plenty.

When once an act is firmly fixed in the mind it has become a habit. Literally millions of people have assigned themselves to poverty or near poverty by the Law of Habit. It has become their habit to spend everything they earn and even worse, a little more.

Therefore, I insist, parents who teach their children the habit of saving are practical and farsighted. The pennies they put in the piggy bank will not amount to much, but it is the habit and personality development that really count.

2. The habit of saving helps you to conserve what you earn, to have something that starts compounding; but more than this, it affects your personality by increasing your vision, initiative, self-confidence and optimism, all of which add to your capacity to earn more. So thrift gets a lot of things going for you.

Get the saving habit. The ant has it, and the Bible commends the work and thrift of the ant to man (Proverbs 6:6-8). In one of Aesop's Fables, he discusses the ant and the grasshopper. In it, he says, "It is thrifty to prepare today for the wants of tomorrow."

Yet, some people have the habit of spending every penny they have, while others have established the habit of putting some back for the future. The Bible calls one group *foolish* and the other *wise* (Proverbs 21:20). It would be interesting, if not shocking, for each to list himself. It might be painful for one to label himself foolish, but it might help him to break the spending habit. If the habit to spend is not broken, a family becomes enslaved to poverty.

HELPS IN ESTABLISHING THE FRUGAL HABIT

In helping you to establish the economical habit, I suggest these basic facts and questions for your consideration:

1. What is not needed is high at any price.

2. Many purchases actually hurt more than they help, give you more to tend and to worry over. Much fretting is found in many unnecessaries.

3. The habit of saving can be just as enjoyable as the habit of spending.

4. If one increases his expenses as much as he increases his income, there is no way to have a surplus.

5. Do I need this *or just think* I do?

6. If I buy it, how much good will I get from it?

7. Will something else that costs less do just as well?

8. Is it priced right?

9. Will there be a better time at a cheaper price to buy it?

10. Debts take what otherwise could be savings. High interest rates. Carrying charges. Extra insurance. What a cruel master debt can be! As the circle gets more vicious, some borrow from Peter to pay Paul, and then borrow from Paul to pay Peter. Like quicksand, the habit of debt pulls a person down deeper and deeper. Nevertheless, I defend some debts, those that are incurred for business and investment purposes; for they are not waste but a ready means of furthering one's assets. But debts made for luxuries are a loss of money and its compounding power to increase.

Some people laugh at the idea that one can become affluent by saving a few dollars a week. As far as their reasoning goes, that may be true, but it does not go far enough. It fails to take into consideration the compounding power of small sums and also the needed capital that small sums can give one to take advantage of business opportunities.

A gentleman at seventy-five who came for a conference with me had already figured that small sums, when compounded, can pile up big. His regret was that he had not put some little savings to work. His was a sad story of what *might have been*. He said, "If I had guarded my spending a few years, I don't mean cutting to the bone — if I had only cut out things that really did not help— I could be a millionaire today, not that I need to be a millionaire at my age, but I do need more than I have."

"How is that?" I replied.

He continued: "If I had saved only $2,000.00 a year from age twenty-five to thirty-five and had allowed it to compound at only 6%, that alone would total today more than $320,000.00.

"Back then we went on a cruise that cost $3,000.00, a part of my inheritance. At 6% compounded interest that totals today $48,000.00. I would have been happier to have stayed at home, for I was sick about half the time. There is no fun in paying $3,000.00 to feed the fish.

"Then there is the yard work, I would have had better health to have done it myself. That would easily total another $64,000.00 if compounded at 6%.

"We thought it seemed fashionable to take our guests to the more expensive eating places when I'm sure that most times it would have been more enjoyable to have dined at home. Let me show you (he had done some figuring) — twenty times in a year at $50.00 a time equals $1,000.00 for the year, and that forty years later at 6% compounded interest equals $16,000.00. And I'm only talking about one year, just one year.

"Furniture was replaced often, and as it was it got more expensive and less comfortable. Drapes got pulled down and replaced to fit changing whims.

"We gave no thought to organizing and coordinating our driving which would have saved expense as well as personal energy. Neither did we try to save on the fuel at home: heating, air conditioning, using the oven, lights or anything else. We were guided by the idea that struck us at the moment.

"Now here I am at seventy-five, broke, unable to get

a job, and my social security is not big enough."

It might have been different if . . . But —

> The saddest words of tongue or pen
> Are these it might have been.

But what might have been for older people *can be* for younger ones, provided they exercise forethought.

You must take the right steps and Step Number Four is: *Be thrifty.* Get the saving habit.

THINK ON THESE THINGS

1. What are the Biblical passages that teach thrift?
2. What are the characteristics of the people referred to in the Bible as "fools"?
3. Describe the stages of economic decline in the story of the Prodigal Son.
4. What is the difference between being thrifty and being a "tightwad"?
5. How can the Law of Habit affect your finances?
6. List some thoughts that you should consider before making purchases.
7. Is it easier to make money or to save money? Why?
8. Discuss areas in which you can learn to save money each week. Decide on the areas most suited to you and your family. Begin making these changes this week.

EIGHT

Have More Coming In
Than You Have Going Out

THE TITLE OF this chapter was my grandmother's expression of a simple rule of economics. I saw the principle work in her life. When grandfather died, she at forty-three was left with six unmarried children. They lived on a farm four miles from a little town. Their living had to come from the soil. No savings, no salary, no social security, no pension, no food stamps. It was up to her and the children and God. But actually that makes a winning team when they work together.

She was not bitter. Neither did she feel sorry for herself. Some more of her philosophy was, "What is *is* and must be accepted." She was practical. She knew she had to play the game of life according to the hand that had been dealt her. It was more profitable to be thankful for what she had than to complain about what she did not have. In memory's storehouse I can still hear her humming and singing as she went about her work.

When I was a little boy I spent considerable time in the summer with grandmother and her children that were still at home. And I learned much from her that no one learns in a classroom. One thing, I observed that when she went to town she always took something to sell. In the fall were the bigger sales of cotton, corn and cattle. But at other times she consistently followed her own economic rule of not going to buy without taking something to sell: butter, cream, eggs, chickens, cured hams, berries, plums, apples, peaches, anything that had a market.

After the years had passed and all the children were married and gone, though she kept the ownership of the farm, she bought a home in town. During my senior year in high school I lived with her, for the village school I had attended did not have the senior year. And when grandmother, at seventy-two went to rest from her labors, she had the 140-acre farm, the home in town and several mortgages she held on farms she had financed for others to buy.

Her simple explanation of her financial success was: "Being I didn't go to school much, I just had to use my head; so I figured that if I had more coming in than I had going out, I would have a surplus." (She had some real humor.) But she used more than her head: her hands, too. They go together real well: a combination of clear thinking and hard work. She didn't have even an elementary school education, but she knew more about finance than some university professors. She knew you have to have more income than expenses, and some of them don't know this, and certainly Washington hasn't learned this lesson.

Have more coming in than you have going out — this is down-to-earth logic from a woman of the soil. You cannot beat that reasoning. For whether you have ten cents or ten million dollars, it is because that principle has been followed. And, to the contrary, when a person has more debts than assets it is because that rule has been violated.

Simple, is it not? And because the principle is so elementary, you may not think that this is a special brainstorm, but you will have to admit that it is a little drizzle that will keep the wolf from the door.

> *There's a whinning at the threshold —*
> *There's a scratching at the floor —*
> *Increase the income or spend less!*
> *The wolf is at the door!*
>
>> *Adapted,*
>> *Charlotte Perkins Stetson Gilman*

So financial well-being demands that we *watch two flows of money: money coming in and money going out.* For finances to accumulate, keep the inflow stream a little larger than the outflow stream.

> *When your outgo exceeds your income, your upkeep is*
> *your downfall.*
>
>> *Executive Digest*

Of course money is not everything, but it is way ahead of bankruptcy.

THE SCRIPTURES

The Scriptures recognize this basic law of inflow-outflow economics!

1. This is seen in a strong act of Joseph. As the food administrator of Egypt and second in command to Pharoah, he gathered food throughout the land during seven plenteous years (Genesis 41). The purpose was to have an adequate supply for the predicted seven years of famine. (How often we have seen one extreme follow another. Wise people take advantage of one to prepare for the other.) The program was so successful that they stored so much grain that they quit numbering it for it

was without number (Genesis 41:49). This was quite a feat made possible by having more coming in than they had going out. It is noteworthy that this was a government measure. Too bad that our own government during the last several years has not seen the wisdom of this economic rule. In a democracy, however, we the people call the shots and maybe we shall learn; if not, our children are sure to wise up . . . when they start paying off our debts.

2. This fundamental of economics is further seen in one of the simple Biblical illustrations we are often using in this book — *the case of the ant* (Proverbs 6:6-11). Along with this divinely given illustration, we are told to "consider her ways, and be wise." The ant rustles more than it eats, and for this reason it has a full storehouse for the winter.

This basic rule of economics — more intake than outgo — can give you plenty. Solomon said:

> So shall thy barns be filled with plenty.
>> Proverbs 3:10

Provided more goes into the barn than is taken out, which requires work and discipline.

Another condition of prosperity given by Solomon is diligence:

> He becometh poor that dealeth with a slack hand: but the hand of the diligent maketh rich.
>> Proverbs 10:4

For he is just as diligent or attentive to preserve as he is to get. His diligence protects the little as well as the big of what he has, for it is his nature.

A LITTLE AT A TIME

The basis of financial progress is a little at a time. However, this is the way all progress is made. Education is achieved a little at a time. A book is written page by page. A house is built brick by brick. A ball game is won play by play. A foot race is won step by step. And, likewise, financial independence is attained act by act whereby you add a little more to your purse than you take out. Your surplus gets bigger and bigger. Financial success is seldom reached in a single act.

Since affluence is achieved in a step-by-step method, then the important questions are: How often are you stepping? And in which direction?

Nevertheless, some say, "When I look at my income versus my expenses, I see no way to get ahead." In all candor, that is negative thinking. You should see not what *is* but what *can be*. Successful people are specialists in positiveness.

INCREASE THE INFLOW

Inasmuch as we have to control the inflow and outflow of money to be prosperous, we note *a few of the many things that can be done to swell the inflow:*

1. Change employment. Switch to one that pays more and has a brighter future. It is very advantageous to start with a young business and grow with it.

2. Take on some extra work. I know a man who worked two extra hours five days a week on another job in a service station. It did not pay much, but it put him on a profitable course. What it paid he would not spend but put it to work earning more. In five years he had a nest egg.

3. I know another man mechanically inclined. To make extra money he started doing little jobs on automobiles of neighbors and friends. Later he quit his regular employment to put in his own garage. Today he has a few mechanics working for him.

4. There is another man I know who took a part time job selling insurance. This extra income enabled him to buy some pieces of property he never would have obtained without it.

5. And there is the man who got a job in the fall gathering pecans. Not only was it a recreational joy for him and his family for several Saturdays, but it was profitable.

6. Many a housewife in her spare time has earned additional money. I am thinking of an expert seamstress who did sewing in her home. She earned enough to pay for a beautiful brick home. Perhaps they never would have gotten it without her help.

7. I know another lady who made enough in house-to-house sales to buy acreage that later skyrocketed in value.

8. Furthermore, I recall the lady who took a job and earned enough to send their son through medical school. By doing this they retained the savings that had been produced by the labors of the husband. They could have sent him to medical school without her working, but it would have reversed their pattern of inflow-outflow economics.

9. There is also the case in which a housewife took an elderly woman into her home and cared for her. The senior lady did not want to go to a nursing home; so she

was better off and so was the younger lady: $25,000.00 better off at the end of five years. If it earns only 6% compounded interest, in twenty years that alone will total $100,000.00, which would be $20,000.00 a year for the five years. Since she likes elderly people and enjoys serving, she said that it enriched her way beyond dollars by giving her the gratifying feeling that her life was a channel of blessing that flowed into the life of a needy person.

10. Likewise, there is the couple that rented a room for half enough to make their house payments.

11. And there is the couple that became house parents in a home for orphans. He continued his regular employment just the same. Since they got free housing, utilities and food, this enabled them to save a large portion of his salary. In a few years they had climbed several rungs on the financial ladder.

I could go on and on citing cases and opportunities, but it would be superfluous. For *where there is a strong desire, the way is found.*

But some tell us, "I don't want to do any of those things." Helpfully, Solomon covers their problem; he teaches that to have an increase one must be willing to do some things that may not at the time be especially to his liking. He said:

> Where no oxen are, the crib is clean; but much increase is by the strength of the ox.
>
> Proverbs 14:4

To have the increase, you must tolerate the ox. You can have a clean crib by not having the ox but not the increase that comes from the ox's labors. You can't have it both ways. If you have the attitude, "I won't put up with this, it's not worth it, I'm not going to have it," then you are not going to have an increasing surplus. *Prosperity has a price;* and if you would have it, you must pay it.

LESSEN THE OUTFLOW

Making money, however, is only half the plan for financial prosperity. *The second half concerns the outflow of it.* And the second is more difficult than the first. For it is easier to make money than it is to keep it. How true:

> He that gets money before it gets wit
> Will be but a short while master of it.

As a grandmother said, "Your dollars go farther when accompanied by sense."

Money has wings and if all you ever see of it is the tail feathers, then you miss the better view.

Therefore, let us briefly weigh *some money-saving techniques:*

1. You can save on almost everything if you watch and time your purchases, especially if you are willing to make substitutes. With all the high prices, it appears that nearly everybody is going to have to do his major shopping during sales.

2. Save the cash in advance for as many purchases as you can. For money talks. Do not let it say *goodbye* without getting due value in return. Furthermore, it saves enormous carrying charges.

3. Conserve the use of utilities. Some have learned that light switches are made to turn off as well as on;

to set the thermostat so there will be no waste; to shut off rooms seldom used; to get full use of electricity and detergents by filling the washing machine and the dishwasher; and to get full value from heating the oven by baking several dishes at the same time.

4. By maintaining your clothes you can dress just as well at half the cost. There is a double benefit in not permitting the children to play in their Sunday clothes: saves the clothes and teaches them to be economical.

5. By planning the meals great savings can be effected. A more expensive dish is not necessarily more delicious or more nutritious. When some foods are seasonably high switch to others. When beef is high and pork low, use more of the latter and vice versa. However, there are many other protein foods to choose from. By figuring costs and making a menu for a week, you can save money, time and yourself from frustration. A lady who did this said, "We're now eating better at 60% of the cost and I'm happier."

6. Cars are expensive to buy and to keep up. So a big saving can come from organizing and coordinating your driving instead of living in the car. When you have to drive two miles and back just to get a loaf of bread it makes the bread expensive. And back again to get some coffee. And then to the cleaners. And then to Mary's to return a magazine. Perhaps all could have been seen after on one trip. See what I mean?

7. In order to save, a family shortened the distance to their vacation spot. They had more fun because they were not on the road so long. Too often we have allowed distance to exert an influence over us beyond its true

value. Distance should have no special charm; it is what is there that counts.

8. I know a family that put in a vegetable garden as a family project. Money was saved. Furthermore, it pulled them together a little tighter and gave them a unity that is lacking in many homes.

9. Another way to cut expenses — I know a family that paints their house inside and outside. All in the family contribute something to the job. It conserves their bank account and gives a personal satisfaction that could not be obtained from hiring it done.

Much more could be said but is unnecessary, for *where there is a will to save, the way is found.*

Inflow and outflow economics — swell the former and lessen the latter. This is Step Number Five.

THINK ON THESE THINGS

1. What did Joseph do to avert a famine in Egypt? How did it relate to inflow-outflow economics?
2. What makes a winning team in the field of economics?
3. How important is it to you to increase your income? Are you willing to pay the price?
4. What are five realistic ways you (and your entire family) can increase the family income?
5. How much of your income will you regularly begin putting into savings now? (Don't fool yourself. It will never be any easier to save money than now.)
6. How many of our expenses are efforts to keep up our

"image" and our "ego"? Are the people we are trying to impress really worth impressing?

7. What are the five most *workable* ways to cut your regular living expenses?

8. How many money saving techniques are we "afraid" to use because of our "image"? Does it *really* matter to anyone else that you eat at less expensive places, drive an older car, etc.?

Seeing Oaks Instead of Acorns

ON A BEAUTIFUL May afternoon thirty years ago two men walked across the same stage and received college diplomas. These two young men were very much alike: good students, ambitious for the future, personable and warm — not intellectually refrigerated.

Recently they returned to their Alma Mater for their thirtieth class reunion.

In spite of the passing thirty years they were still very much alike: personable, married with children and pursuers of the same occupation.

But there was a difference.

One owned his own company. The other was still working for a company, receiving an average salary.

What made the difference? Undoubtedly, drive played a big part, but perhaps the most determining factor was vision, seeing ahead or imagination. One saw opportunities and possibilities the other did not see.

POWER OF VISION

When Andrew Carnegie was asked the secret of his remarkable success, he replied, "I owe it all to my flashes." Farsighted flashes that he executed. Perhaps all of us at times have some flashes that have possibilities; we should analyze them, discard the impractical ones, and put into effect the sound ones.

1. What we see will have a great effect on what we get. Successful people have a long and clear vision. The Bible clearly sets forth the sure failure of those who have not this dynamic power:

> Where there is no vision, the people perish.
> Proverbs 29:18

However, we do not have to be devoid of vision, for it is one thing no person has a monopoly on. Nobody has a corner on creative thinking. In this wide world there are opportunities out there to be seen by all who will open their eyes and look. This is the injunction Jesus gave:

> Lift up your eyes, and look on the fields.
> John 4:35

Yes, Jesus gave the precept relative to spiritual seeing; but the right to look in secular areas is also open to all, and absolutely essential if one would see.

2. Vision is actually mind power or thought control; and, since success begins in the mind, this fundamental bearing on man's future cannot be over-emphasized. Definitely, *the doors of success swing on the hinges of thought,* and thus open or close in keeping with a person's thinking. The Bible is plain on the point that man is what he thinks:

> For as he thinketh in his heart, so is he.
> Proverbs 23:7

Inasmuch as *thinking is a forerunner of success,* you need to have a brainstorm once in a while, not just the same old cloudy mist. This will get you out of the rut. You can go down the rut without thinking; but to get out, you must think. And he who doesn't is doomed to mediocrity.

Indeed, for our scatter-brain-thinking, which we sometimes do, we have to pay. Our snap-judgments which cause us to decide on courses discordant with logic are the result of tangent thought waves related to unreal imagination. So keep your thinking on a straight course.

Just like the oak develops from the germ in the acorn, human achievement develops out of systematic plans that come from the *imagination*. First, there is the thought; second, there is the organization of the thought into plans; and third, there is the execution of the plans into reality.

3. In addition to being creative, vision or imagination is also *interpretative*. After examining facts, it conceives and creates new associations and plans out of them. This is actually putting an old idea into a new use. This is what Clarence Saunders, the grocery clerk, did in launching the help-yourself grocery stores. The idea struck him while he was standing in a cafeteria line. It dawned on him that if self-help would work in a cafeteria, it would also work in a grocery store. His imagination paid off.

WHAT ABOUT YOUR VISION?

1. Do you see possibility or impossibility? I hope it is the former, for blessed is the person who sees possibility with a challenge. The view of attainableness turns a person loose to achieve what he sees, but a pic-

ture of impossibility stops one where he is. All success is predicated on a positive attitude.

2. Are you seeing the facts?

> Ye shall know the truth, and the truth shall make you free.
>
> John 8:32

When you see and believe something misleading, you are going to be misled. Be not deceived by false appearances. There is no water in a mirage. Illusions can break you. Do not underestimate the problems you face nor the competition you have, but rather see the true state of affairs.

3. Are you allowing your sight of the present to preclude your view of the future? It can!

This was demonstrated by a wise old Indian. He held an acorn before his two sons and asked: "What do you see?" One said, "An acorn." The other answered, "An oak." To the second the father commented, "With your vision, some day you should be chief."

Seeing only the present is hurting a lot of people. Not being able to look beyond their present paycheck and fringes, they will never advance very far. They are so determined to get *now,* (so set on not giving one minute nor doing one thing extra) that they set up their own roadblock that bars their future progress.

The sight of one fast buck has caused a lot of people to lose sight of a thousand. Trying to make a *kill* on one deal can kill you.

4. Indeed, we can become so engrossed in one thing that we cannot see anything else. We can become like

the little girl on the train who was absorbed with one thought. When the conductor picked up her ticket he said, "You're going to Seattle." She quickly replied, "No, I'm going to see grandma." Figuratively, we can be so obsessed in going to see *grandma* that we can't go to Se-attle.

Many are so concerned and busy seeing what it takes to make a living that they cannot see what it takes to become affluent.

5. Also, a person can allow himself to stand in the way of his own vision. There is a whole new world out there, and to see it we have to look beyond self.

This is why granny failed in her little cafe. She thought everybody liked what she liked. Too much cornbread, turnips and cabbage.

> Look not every man on his own things, but every man also on the things of others.
>
> Philippians 2:4

6. Now, here is another pertinent question: Are you allowing tradition to lock your vision into the old and to obstruct it to anything new? This can hurt you both spiritually and materially.

> Thus have ye made the commandment of God of none effect by your tradition.
>
> Matthew 15:6

Don't let the ruts of traditional thinking blind you to a bigger world.

Poor John, however, is a traditional thinker and liver. A disciple of routine. He goes to work over the same road, does the very same work in the precise manner, returns home the unchanging way, at the invariable time. On arrival he greets his wife the same trite way: "What's cookin'?" He then eats dinner at the same time, takes his shower at the usual time, then sits in the same chair, reads the same sections of the same paper until he dozes at the customary time, and then gets up and goes to bed at the regular time. And the next morning he starts the same routine all over again. He is so routine that I have thought that if the clock of the universe should stop, we could set it by taking a look at John. He has not had a new thought in ten years. No vision. Tradition and routine have boxed him in. And boredom is engulfing him fast.

It is evident therefore that if one would get more vision and wider perspective, he must get out of his routine. Associate with some new people. If you restrict your associations to only those in your own valley of interest, you are not apt to see on the other side of the mountain. Also, read some new materials. Go to some different places. And be sure to give yourself some time everyday to be alone to think.

7. Here is another helpful question: Are you seeing too many roadblocks to be successful? This is what stops many. They see:

1) A little self. Those who depreciate themselves are doomed to mediocrity. They get hung up on a few come-easy statements like these: "I would like to but . . ." "My talent is lacking." "The good opportunities have been taken." "No need to try, I would fail."

Some people see themselves as poor and always poor. But one thing that distinguishes man from the animal is his ability to improve his lot.

2) Some see the mass of humanity as crooks. This limits their business activity. You will prosper more if you see people as upright, honest creatures instead of scoundrels.

Oh yes, I have been taken to a cleaning several times. It began happening early in life. When I was sixteen I had a little money that mostly came the hard way. But Deacon Didn't Pay needed money for his family, he said; furthermore, he promised me interest which I needed. So I lent him $100.00 (equal to about $2,000.00 now) which I had planned to use that fall in college. He gave me a note to make me feel real secure — his name was on it. And before that note came due I was already feeling a little remorse at the thought of taking interest from a man who needed money for his family. But that little gnawing of distress was very much in vain, because I didn't have to worry about taking that interest — not even the principal. You see, I began to learn about being "trimmed" in the School of Experience while I was in my teens. As you would expect, warm friends gave me the cold and customary consolation: "You can't take it with you." And I must admit that I never knew before that "taking it with you" meant "taking it to college."

Still, I have a lot of faith in mankind — yes, maybe a little more in a tiptop sinner than I have in a second class saint. That $100.00, however, was not lost: It — as well as all subsequent clippings — was an investment in a broader education than any college has to offer. There is no greater book of learning than the *Book of Experience*. There you get to meet the authors. And, believe me, I've met a few. I could go on and on. So don't tell me that a book like this on *Living on the Plus*

Side is not needed. Too bad, at least for me, that the deacon and some others had not had such a course. Yet, I still believe that the great majority of the people are good. And I am glad I have that trust. For the business world largely operates on the basis of faith in mankind — not blind faith but trust based on some evidences. With a leaning toward faith in people you will find that they are *crowds with silver linings.*

3) Are you one of the many that see only an overcrowded field? "The field is so crowded now that they're walking on each other" is their oft-repeated statement that raises a white flag. They give up before they try.

4) There are others who see nothing but minimal security. "I've got a little living where I am; better not give it up; a bird in the hand is worth a hundred in the bush." What they are saying is "goodbye" to all opportunities for better things.

5) And some others can see only family dependence. "I can't change because I've got a family," is the killing remark of a pessimist. But the optimist says, "I must change because I've got a family."

Unmistakably, what you see will have a bearing on where you go. If you see only roadblocks, you will be stopped dead in your tracks.

8. Summed up, do you see opportunities? You must if you would find a fast current to carry you into the ocean of plenty.

> *There is a tide in the affairs of men*
> *Which, taken at the flood, leads on to fortune;*
> *Omitted, all the voyage of their life*
> *Is bound in shallows and in miseries.*
>
> William Shakespeare

Opportunities have always existed and always will in a free economy. Nevertheless, some remark, "All the good opportunities are gone; if I had lived only fifty years sooner." The time in which you live, however, is not as important as how wide you open your eyes.

Be sure your eyes are open wide enough to see opportunities for *yourself* — not that restricted view that sees only what *others* could do. Isn't it strange how that some people can see big mammoth undertakings for the other fellow but not for themselves? Along this line, a small man said to a large man, "If I were your size, I would go out into the forest and find the biggest bear there and give him a whipping like nobody has ever seen." The big man replied, "Mister, there are still a lot of little bears in the forest."

As Step Number Six, *lift up your eyes.* See an opportunity and hitch your wagon to it.

THINK ON THESE THINGS

1. What does the Bible say about vision?
2. How can selfishness and tradition cloud our vision of the future?
3. How may you allow your vision of the present to block your vision of the future?
4. Exercise your creative, visionary skills. See yourself as you want to be in one year, five years.
5. How may our own likes and dislikes interfere with seeing opportunities.
6. Who are the most optimistic people you know? Begin associating with them as much as possible.

7. Get out of some ruts this week. Try some new approaches to everyday situations. Do something that's really fun!
8. Affirm yourself. Talk to yourself this week. You are a winner. You deserve to be successful.

TEN

Three Miles and Six Cents

A BASIC CHAPTER in the book of *Living on the Plus Side* of financial success is Honesty. Unless you master this chapter the other chapters are meaningless. For honesty is as indispensable to financial progress as legs are to a runner; without it you will not run far nor last long.

1. Indeed, *much of the art of successful business dealings is found in being honest,* because confidence is essential to trade. And —

> *Confidence . . . thrives only on honesty, on honor, on the sacredness of obligations.*
>
> *Franklin D. Roosevelt*

Honesty covers many faults; and if a man has this quality, we are willing to carry on commerce with him, notwithstanding he has some traits we don't like.

The Bible, the history of man and common sense, all three, tell us that honesty — a quality that is above cheating, stealing or misrepresentation — pays. The universal recognition of its value has given rise to the maxim:

> *Honesty is the best policy.*

However, *honesty is more than a policy.* It is a principle, and as such is a Guiding Star to success. Honesty for the sake of expediency, however, is not honesty — just opportunism devoid of conviction, which may flip-flop for a greater reward. But real honesty lasts, for it is deep-seated — not convenience.

When honesty is a principle it unquestionably adds to a person's character a necessary element which makes for achievement. It works like this: It gives a person a sense of integrity that allows him to hold high his head in self-respect, and begins a chain of causation of earned success. And if he should become the victim of outright lies or distorted truths, he knows he is honest. This gives him heart. Furthermore, what a person knows of himself and how he sees himself is apt to be the way the world sees him.

A number of qualities contributed to the greatness and success of Abraham Lincoln, but perhaps none contributed as much as his uncompromising and unflagging honesty. It has been reported that when he was in the grocery business, he once discovered that he had made a mistake of charging a customer six cents too much. That night when he closed the store he walked three miles and returned the six cents. Many such incidents in Lincoln's life won for him the affectionate title: *Honest Abe.*

Honesty pays but apparently to dishonest people it does not pay enough; though they do not see it, their dishonesty pays less and less with every crooked deal. For there is a tongue in every fraudulent transaction that cries out, "No more!" Business drops off with every false move. Even the cheats themselves are repelled, knowing that if they do business with a filcher they are likely to be fleeced.

Indeed, *dishonesty is a peep-hole on man* that lets others see him as he is. And what they see, they do not like. They are turned off. People who work hard and economize stringently are not going to intentionally roll their dollars down a crooked path. The straight and narrow way is much more inviting.

All are mortal and may err, but it is so foolish for the error to be dishonesty. For man can climb much higher by being on the level.

THE BIBLE SPEAKS

1. In God's plan for financial success honesty is a *MUST*. And equivocally —

> *"By hook or by crock"*
> *Is not by the Book.*

For the Bible says:

> Let us walk honestly.
> Romans 13:13

Every violation of this command is a sure way to lose credibility in the commercial world. If you doubt this, just look around. If there are any you suspect of crookedness, you do not care to carry on trade with them.

Instead, we prefer people with a conscience. We pick those who have the attitude expressed by Paul in the Bible:

> We trust we have a good conscience, in all things willing to live honestly.
> Hebrews 13:8

We do not have to read a book on business to know that

we had rather patronize a person or a firm with a conscience. Clearly, those who have it have an advantage over those devoid of it.

2. In the strongest moral code ever formulated — *The Ten Commandments* — we have this rule which protects personal possessions.

> Thou shalt not steal.
>
> Exodus 20:15

There are several ways this rule can be violated: one is with a gun; another is with a lie; and no one can say the former is worse than the latter. Taking another's possession at his back is theft; likewise, taking something at his face through misrepresentation is theft; and failing to pay a debt is also thievery. A thief is a thief regardless of the method he uses. In any case, it violates the ethics and morals necessary to sustain society — and successful trade. Hence, for the formation of a better person and the protection of society, the Bible rings with this command:

> But let none of you suffer as a murderer, or as a thief.
>
> I Peter 4:15

Because this old-time moral code which respects the person, the rights and the possessions of another are being disregarded by many, our society is now suffering nightmares. And I mean literal nightmares. A drive through the streets is very revealing: bars on residential windows, burglar alarms, and people going in groups for protection. How horrifying is the thought of a world of thieves!

While swindling is a more sophisticated way to steal than breaking in, the results are the same for the loser.

Takes less courage than using a gun. A little more refined. But it is still theft. Furthermore, it is perpetrated by lying and this adds more speed to a sure way to wreck a business. Any apparent business success resulting from lies and deceits is short-lived. So the following command is not to boss us but to help us:

> A false balance is abomination to the Lord: but a just weight is his delight.
>
> Proverbs 11:1

An abomination to the Lord! And to man also — if he knows it, and in time he learns it.

A man in the filling station business changed his pumps to give a shortage. It was bad business. It irritates the customer to put twenty-three gallons in a twenty-two gallon tank.

Inasmuch as *wealth is made in relationship to others,* then anything that interferes with the association of others hinders the accumulation of wealth. Dishonesty does. Thus dishonesty is a detriment to becoming wealthy. A reputation for honesty is an invaluable asset in your climb to financial success. Every man who plans to stay in business should learn the value of this Scripture:

> Provide things honest [honorable] in the sight of all men.
>
> Romans 12:17

4. The positive approach to business found in truth, honesty and justice is much more productive than the seeming shortcuts of falsehood, dishonesty and injustice. Thus, here are some essential rules for business success and beautiful living:

Whatsoever things are true,
Whatsoever things are honest,
Whatsoever things are just,
Whatsoever things are pure,
Whatsoever things are lovely,
Whatsoever things are of good report,
. . . think on these things.

Philippians 4:8

This passage prohibits even thinking along the lines of
how to overcharge, beat a bill, defraud and deceive.

THE GOLDEN RULE

Summed up, *the best business rule is the Golden
Rule.* As it makes a person trustworthy and acceptable,
it gives him a magnetism that draws others to him.
Nobody has ever come up with better public relations
than that wrapped up in the Golden Rule, which says:

Therefore all things whatsoever you would that men
should do unto you, do ye also unto them.

Matthew 7:12

There is a law of operation that says we reap what
we sow. As your dealings bless or harm others, they
finally return to bless or harm you. If there is anything
fully attested in the Bible (and there is), it is the fact
that man is the reaper of what he sows, both spiritually and materially. This is one of the sure and irrevocable
laws of the universe. Understand it and you are on your
way to noble ethics, reciprocal principles and consequently greater success. Some may say this is an old-fashioned
idea; and I grant that it is old, but in workability it is
as new as tomorrow.

To prove that it still works, I ask: Which do you
prefer, a Golden Rule lawyer or an Iron Rule lawyer?

A Golden Rule store or an Iron Rule store? A Golden Rule repairman or an Iron Rule repairman? A Golden Rule mechanic or an Iron Rule mechanic? Which doctor had you rather have to decide if you need surgery, a Golden Rule doctor or an Iron Rule doctor? As we think of the built-in success of the Golden Rule, we wonder why everybody cannot see to follow it. This rule is not only golden in ethics but also in reciprocity wherein gold comes to its doer. Indeed, the Golden Rule has financial rewards.

A passive belief in the Golden Rule, however, offers nothing; it is only when you follow it that you put in motion the good things that come back to you. And if it is only superficially used as a cloak to try to hide a different self, it puts a person in the unhappy state of being at odds with himself which later puts him in discord with others. But when this rule is actually a part of one's being, he is seen as a person worthy of patronage and trust. Such recognition has to help.

Furthermore, the Golden Rule blesses because of what it does for its follower. When it is imbibed in your very nature, it has a tendency to give you a positive, dynamic personality. You think positively, not negatively. You have no thought nor time for petty jealousies, cold retaliations and hostile maneuvers that sap energy and restrict labors. Free of all this, there is a bigger and more beautiful world out there to work — all because you are bigger and more beautiful yourself.

It is true that some people do not respond in kind to the good you do them, but it is still profitable to the doer because the act affects his own sub-conscious mind. And this is a powerful source of profit. You may go a long time before there is any reciprocation from others for your Golden Rule dealings, but nevertheless it is adding strength and animation into the formation of a positive character. This is the better reason for fairness and justice — not what it may cause others to do for you but what it may do to your own character.

Truly, the world could stand a mighty big dose of the Golden Rule just now. In it are new hopes and new reapings to supply the material wants and moral relations of mankind.

So I insist: *rugged honesty and Golden Rule principles are essential to financial success.* I must hold to this thesis or else be forced to believe our society has gone mad. So, Step Number Seven — *be honest.*

THINK ON THESE THINGS

1. What does the Bible say about honesty?
2. Who says honesty pays? Do you really believe that?
3. How is wealth made in relationship to others?
4. How can a reputation for honesty aid one in financial success?
5. Are your business dealings and personal relationships completely honest?
6. How does following the Golden Rule affect you as well as the ones you come in contact with?
7. What are the subtle, less noticeable forms of dishonesty?
8. What can be done to encourage greater honesty among your associates and friends? Your family and your children?

ELEVEN

Look to Tomorrow

INVESTING IN THE future has to begin today. We must look to tomorrow. Furthermore, whether we realize it or not, *nearly everyone believes in and has financial investments.*

NEARLY EVERYBODY IS FOR INVESTMENTS

I know the vast majority of religious bodies and their ministers believe in investments for they have pensions or go in on Social Security.

A *pension* is made possible by a subtraction from a person's pay plus an addition by the employer. If no pension were provided, the employee could now receive each payday an increase equal to both amounts without increasing the expense of the employer. It is a present investment in the hope of future returns.

The same is true of *Social Security*, for it is an investment program initiated and made binding by the government. It is a current investment for an eventual reaping. Its widespread participation is sure proof the American people rely on investments.

Life insurance is more evidence that millions of our people like the idea of investing capital to get returns. The chief appeal of this particular investment is that small sums can provide large amounts for one's family at a critical time in the event the bread winner's life is cut short.

Also, there are the millions of home owners and holders of other *real estate* who bought in the hope of some kind of gain and security.

Furthermore, our *material way of life* largely rests on investments. The food we eat, the clothes we wear, the cars we drive, the televisions we watch, the electricity we burn, the gas we consume, the carpets that cover our floors, the stoves on which we cook, etc., etc., are the products from investments. The capital was invested by stockholders to produce the goods in anticipation of reaping returns. It is impossible to realize what life would be like without investments.

LOGIC SUPPORTS INVESTMENTS

Logic also supports the right to make investments. To argue that one can reap money from his toil but cannot reap money from the money his toil produces is absurd. *If one works for money, it is only fair that his money later work for him.*

Since it is evident that most people believe in investments — Social Security and pensions are examples — let us carry the thought a little further: Suppose some people prefer to start reaping before they reach retirement age. Then they must make other investments. Logic says that if Social Security and pensions are permissible and even desirable, then so are other investments calculated to pay dividends sooner. The principle is that of receiving dividends from invested money, and the timing is not the determining factor in the right or wrong of it. Suppose some people should want more than either Social Security or pensions can provide, then they must make other investments. It violates reason to say that one is permissible and the other is not. It defies sound thinking to say that a senior citizen can have one hamburger but not two, one room but not two. Truly, consistency cries out that if it is right to make investments which return the bare necessities, it is also right to make more investments which return more dividends.

Logic is on the side of investments; the people are for them; and in the third place the Scriptures sustain them.

INVESTMENTS RECORDED IN THE BIBLE

1. In the Parable of the Talents, *Jesus spoke of two kinds of money-handlers:* the wise investor and the fearful hoarder (Matthew 25:14-27). As you read the Scripture given, bear in mind that a talent was a large sum of money — not an ability as we commonly use the word today. In the story a certain master gave to three servants different sums to invest. The man given five talents doubled his capital — gained five; the man entrusted with two talents doubled his wealth — gained two; but the man given one talent "went and digged in the earth, and hid" the money. Later the capable investors were commended by their master, but the frightened steward was censured. The master said that the buried money at least could have been put on interest and earned a little — not just left to lie there earning nothing. While Jesus told this story to teach a spiritual lesson on the use of abilities, it also gives us a lesson on material investments — and a good one.

2. One of the more popular investments spoken of in the Bible is in *land.* Of course, there were not as many kinds of investments available then as today.

Concerning real estate: Abraham bought the field of Machpelah and the field of Ephron (Genesis 49:30).

"And Jacob . . . bought a parcel of a field . . . for a hundred pieces of money" (Genesis 33:18,19). This land later became "the inheritance of the children of Joseph," Jacob's grandchildren (Joshua 24:32).

Also, Jeremiah purchased Hanameel's field: "And I bought the field of Hanameel my uncle's son, that was in Anathoth, and weighed him the money, even seventeen shekels of silver. And I subscribed the evidence, and sealed it, and took witness, and weighed him the money in the balances" (Jeremiah 32:9,10). It is interesting to observe that Jeremiah took steps to assure the title of the property.

Additionally, we read in the Bible that Boaz was "a mighty man of wealth" who had investments in real estate (Ruth 2:1,2).

3. Interestingly, another kind of investment in that early day was in *livestock.* Famous examples are that of Abraham and Lot who had more cattle than grazing which precipitated strife between their herdsmen. The trouble was settled, however, by a gracious gesture on the part of Abraham in permitting his nephew Lot to choose the land he wanted and then Abraham went in the opposite direction (Genesis 13:1-12).

4. Abraham was also an investor in *silver and gold* (Genesis 13:1,2).

5. Still another type of investment spoken of in the Scriptures is *precious jewels:* "Again, the kingdom of heaven is like unto a merchantman, seeking goodly pearls: who when he had found one pearl of great price, went and sold all that he had, and bought it" (Matthew 13:46). Indeed, Jesus related this to teach a spiritual lesson, but it also tells us of investments in that day.

Inasmuch as investments can lose as well as gain, then it is very relevant to recall that Job lost a fortune and gained it back twice as big (Job 1:3, 14-22; 42:12,13).

THE RIGHT OF INDIVIDUAL OWNERSHIP AND INVESTMENT

It is evident *the Bible teaches the right of individual ownership and personal investment.*

It is true that some church members in the first century sold possessions and shared with the needy to meet an economic emergency, but it is also true that it was neither compulsory nor the act of a communal organization. Instead, it was an act of benevolence.

This is obvious in the sale of some land owned by Ananias and Sapphira. Concerning it, Peter said, "While it remained, was it not thine own? and after it was sold, was it not in thine own power?" (Acts 5:4). It was theirs (not the church's), and after it was sold the money was theirs (not the church's), and they had the right to do with it as they saw fit. No commune. Instead, individual ownership.

Of course, the church cared for widows and other needy persons, but this was benevolence — not common ownership. Not all widows, however, were supported by the church — only the widows described as "widows indeed" (I Timothy 5:5,16). It was commanded that all other widows be supported by their families that the church be not charged (I Timothy 5:16). This is proof that the church was not a communal organization with a common treasury that supported all its members.

Individual ownership with its possibility of growth motivates man to greater activity. It gives him a feeling of accomplishment, security and well-being. Some contend, however, that under communal ownership in which everybody owns everything the same feeling derived from personal ownership is engendered. In all candor, this is not so. If you doubt it, ask the farmer if he has the same feeling of ownership toward the ocean that he has toward his private lake.

Indeed, *the Bible concept of man is one of freedom,* internal and external. Man was given a soul which is all his own (Genesis 2:7). This gives him an internal freedom that no one else can exercise. Tyrants may make him bend in body, but he possesses the freedom of the soul which enables him to think and feel internally as he pleases. He does not have to answer to anyone for his exercise of this freedom, except to the One who gave it to him — Almighty God.

A man is free on the inside because he has something there he can call his own — his soul; likewise, he is free on the outside because he has something there he can call his own — property. The possession of property is therefore only the outward manifestation of what a man possesses within — freedom, complete freedom.

This freedom of man to pursue his own economic course is a liberty from the hand of God (Ecclesiastes 2:24).

TYPES OF INVESTMENTS

There is no set formula for investments that fits everybody's personal need. What is good for one may be bad for another. Thus the type of investment should vary with ages and circumstances. The young can afford to take more risks than the aged, for if the investments fail they have more time for a comeback.

Remember — *your ship will not come in unless you send it out.*

Whatever the investments, it is wise to *start making them as soon as possible.* For most investments need time to start multiplying. Dragging your feet can keep you from arriving. So do not wait too late.

> *While we wait for the napkin, the soup*
> *gets cold,*
> *While the bonnet is trimming, the face*
> *grows old,*
> *When we've matched our buttons, the*
> *pattern is old,*
> *And everything comes too late — too late.*
>
> *Fitzhugh Ludlow*

Furthermore, *the wise investor seeks counsel.* However, unless the counselors are wise and knowledgeable, one is no better off — maybe worse. It is easy to get the wrong advice, especially up and down the streets. So do not listen to the unsuccessful.

> Where no counsel is, the people fall: but in the multitude of counselors there is safety.
>
> Proverbs 11:14

After consulting counselors, in the last analysis you will have to make the decision. So think it through. Personally, I like to sleep on a proposition; it may have a different look in the morning. This gives me a little more time to look before I leap.

I recall the story of the cowboy, vexed with a rash, who ran and jumped into a cactus plant. Later his classic explanation was, "Well, at the time it seemed like it was the thing to do."

We laugh at the cowboy because actually we are laughing at ourselves. For most of us have at times jumped too fast. I have. Perhaps you have.

It comes down to this: *the best investor is the person with the best judgment.*

> *Men's judgments are a parcel of their fortunes.*
> *William Shakespeare*

In recent years some have done well in *real estate,* while others have lost. But I have seen the "boom" and the "bust" in real estate. In the Great Depression I saw my father sell good farming land close to town for $8.00 an acre. While real estate — like anything else — has had its ups and downs, as a whole it has a long history of appreciation and has been a considerable hedge against inflation.

So have stocks in *good companies.* They are, however, more vulnerable to ups and downs. For ordinarily they do not sell according to value but according to the moods and emotions of the people. But stocks in the right companies that have been ridden through the lows have proved to be profitable and a lift to offset inflation. A good rule to follow in the stock market is to buy when everybody wants to sell and to sell when everybody wants to buy. It takes nerve and courage to do this, but it usually works.

Bonds, both corporate and municipal, provide a stipulated return. But there is the problem of inflation which is now giving the financial world a bad headache and an ulcerated stomach. The same problem exists concerning money on interest in banks and in savings and loan companies. You cannot gain on money you lend when the inflation rate is as high as the interest you receive.

The cruel, thievish hands of inflation reach into every person's cash and steal the fruits of his hard earned labors. It is the meanest and most deceptive kind of robbery. For instance, if a person receives $60.00 interest on $1,000.00 and if he pays 25% in income taxes, he has a net interest of $45.00; but if the inflation rate is 6%, then his $1,000.00 loses $60.00 in true value while it earns $45.00, which means the unfortunate investor actually loses $15.00 a year on his investment. We need to bear in mind that the dollar has a value and we have witnessed its rapid devaluation.

I have two bills that tell a story. I got them out of my bank box three years ago, framed them and hung them on my office wall just to remind me of what inflation will do. I have owned these bills for forty-two years. One bill is 50,000 German marks, dated 1922; the other is 100,000 German marks, dated 1923. When that money was printed, World War I had been over four and five years. There should have been stability. Instead, the German government pursued a course that accelerated inflation. Their view was, "We don't have to worry; we have a printing press." And they kept it busy. Inflation reached such proportions that it took a roll of bills to buy a cup of coffee and later the currency became completely worthless. The government fell with all its earthshaking reverberations. I hope we learn. I hope America learns.

Indeed, the history of governments throughout the world is proof that currency is not always safe.

For a nation to employ an economic formula that continually steals from its people by decreasing the value of their money is the most ruthless miscarriage of human justice. Every government is destined to fail and every economic principle will run aground in shame, if it does not provide reasonable stability for its currency.

What I have said about inflation is not pessimistic but realistic. It needs to be said because every investor should be realistic — not a pessimist but a realist with a positive drive. So, *invest wisely* — Step Number Eight.

THINK ON THESE THINGS

1. What does the Bible say about investments?
2. Why do we know that most churches believe very strongly in investments?
3. Some people have said they do not need investments because they trust in God. Is this sound reasoning?
4. Who is the best investor?
5. How does inflation steal from the people?
6. Without using the rent money or the mortgage money, how much can you save or invest weekly or monthly?

7. What investments are best suited to your finances at present? Remember, you may begin slowly, step-by-step, but you *must* begin. Check out all the opportunities first.
8. Teach your family about investments. What small investments can your children (or other young people in your family) begin to make?

TWELVE

Today's Worthy Woman

THERE IS NO WAY to discuss *Living on the Plus Side* of life without giving full recognition and credit to a wife's role. God placed her by the side of man, and her part in the partnership is of immense significance. She is his surest partner and safest steward. In fact, *of all the simple means to financial success, a good wife is the best.* Hence, the day a man chooses a wife is the day he chooses, at least to some extent, his financial future. For the wife is the keeper of the home (I Timothy 2:5), and how she keeps it will have great bearing on the economic success of the family. In the average family she determines how and where much of the money is spent. If she is a discerning, thrifty economist, it can make a bankroll of difference.

So some women marry poor men and help them to become rich, while some other women marry rich men and help them to become poor.

Any man with an average annual income and a wife with a huge annual spending habit is in trouble. The family is soon covered with a mountain of problems. Overworked spending habits put a family in financial chains and enslave them to outside masters. All because of debts! Indeed, the wife can do much to create the "spending habit" or to prevent it. If the mother cannot

stand for money to accumulate — burns her pocket — it
is mighty easy for everybody in the family to develop
the same attitude. And with that burn-it-up view it soon
goes, that is until the laws of economics catch up with
them; and rest assured, sooner or later they will. Spending should be done to bless a family, but the "spending
habit" is an uncontrolled urge which brings hardships
and miseries

There is a strong desire in the human heart to have
plenty in this life. Don't let the "spending habit" keep
it from being realized. For he who spends too much today will have less to spend tomorrow.

Thus if a wife does a good job in aiding the financial standing of the family, her husband certainly ought
to heed the advice of Billy Sunday who said:

> Try praising your wife, even if it does frighten
> her at first.

It is true that some men can make it without a
woman's help, but think how much easier it is and how
much higher he can go if he has a wife who is helpful.

Knowing the power of womanhood, companies prefer
that their highest ranking workers have the highest
ranking wives. Unquestionably, it is an invaluable asset
for a man to have a wife who is in sympathy with him
and in tune with his aspirations.

Indeed, the smart, mature, unselfish wife can do
much to keep her husband in the positive, optimistic,
cheerful mood which is so necessary to financial attainment. Anything that irritates him and stirs up anger
and cynicism within him takes its toll from his full productive powers. So it is easy to see how that different

wives can produce different results in husbands. One can contribute to his irritation, unambition and impoverishment, while another can inspire him to have a winning outlook.

Woman's role in which she tends the household and enhances the finances of a family is so momentous that Solomon pays the most renowned tribute in all literature to her worthiness. He states that she is more valuable than rubies, meaning that she is more precious than any material possession. From the record in Proverbs 31:10-31 we observe:

1. The worthy wife is an asset to her husband. "She will do him good and not evil all the days of her life" (v. 12). A source of help — not a detriment. She pursues his best interest in both good and bad times.

2. She seeks materials for clothing and household needs and works them gladly with her hands. "She seeketh wool, and flax, and worketh willingly with her hands" (v. 13). She honors the universal law of work by working. Not only does she work, she works joyfully. This is a major accomplishment. For unwilling work can condition a person to become an irritant nagger, but this woman is spared such for she enjoys her work.

3. She gives thought and attention to set the best table possible, even at times obtaining food from a distance. "She is like the merchants' ships; she bringeth her food from afar" (v. 14). Without regard to distance, she buys the best bargains. Her domestic duties are performed expertly. She knows that —

> *Kissing don't last; cookery do.*
> *George Meredith*

She has trained herself to be an excellent cook, for she also knows —

> *There is one thing more exasperating than a wife who can cook and won't, and that's the wife who can't cook and will.*
>
> Robert Frost

4. She is industrious and energetic. "She riseth also while it is yet night and giveth meat [food] to her household, and a portion [their task] to her maidens" (v. 15). She rises before dawn to get on with her daily work. Obviously, her husband in the morning is not sent off to encounter the world with nothing but a broken snore from her. Indeed, it means much for a man to have an assuring, appreciative send-off in the morning. It gives him a little extra strength to succeed.

5. In addition to her thrift, she actually earns extra income. "She considereth a field, and buyeth it: with the fruit of her hands she planteth a vineyard" (v. 16). Her industry, prudence and thrift provide the means to increase her operations. She saves money. She makes money. She is successful. It is noteworthy that in this Biblical presentation of the ideal wife we do not see a destitute domestic travailing in wretched poverty. Instead, we see a prosperous, comfortable home in which the wife's efforts have made a great difference. Neither does the chapter picture woman as an idle ornament to be kept like a flower in a hothouse. Idleness has never increased any woman's femininity and beauty. To the contrary, it produces frustration and restlessness, increases physical ailments, dulls personality and fades beauty. This has often happened to women in what is called the "affluent classes." Obviously, God never cut

out either sex for a life of indolence. Neither does the Book of Proverbs confine a wife's duties to only her own household. Contrariwise, in addition to her household tasks, she is a manufacturer, a merchant, a landowner and a farmer. While a woman's main occupation is to keep the home, it also needs to be observed that it is permissible and honorable for her to engage in any other occupations her time, talent and health will permit.

6. Because of the conditions she has met, she has the pleasure of profitable enterprises. "She perceiveth that her merchandise is good [profitable]" (v. 18). Hard work, thoughtful thrift and good judgment leave her with a surplus profit which brings satisfaction. Thus a profit-making business, operated by man or woman, is Biblical and legitimate, a rightful reward from duly invested capital and labor. Profit ought not therefore to be kicked around as something unlawful and evil. Truly, the profit-making incentive keeps the commercial world humming.

7. She also works as the need dictates rather than as the clock ticks. "Her candle goeth not out by night" (v. 18). It was an ancient custom to keep a candle burning at night, but in this context it relates to her diligence and industry which suggests night work. In tribute to her long hours it has been truthfully stated:

> *Man may work from sun to sun,*
> *But woman's work is never done.*
>
> *Anonymous*

8. Moreover, she renders money-saving services that otherwise would cost her husband much. "She layeth her hands to the spindle, and her hands hold the distaff" (v. 19). She knows that a dollar saved is more than a

dollar made. Thus it is very understandable why the family is prosperous. It is not practical today, however, to take hold of the clumsy spindle and outmoded distaff, but the spirit that did in ancient times is practical today and can be applied to more modern means. Her slavish tools therefore need changing but not her willing spirit.

9. Furthermore, she keeps her house and herself in the best appearance. "She maketh herself coverings of tapestry; her clothing is silk and purple" (v. 22). She was not dressing above her station — she made her station. Indeed, the more valuable garb for any woman is that which clothes her inner nature, spoken of in verse twenty-five — "Strength and honor are her clothing" — but this does not argue that she should not be concerned with fine and attractive clothing for her body. We see from this passage that it is not wrong nor unscriptural for a woman to dress in silks and satins. As I have said before, I say again — *man the best of God's creation should not be expected to live on the worst.*

10. Being a manufacturer of more than her family's needs, she sells what she can. "She maketh fine linen, and selleth it; and delivereth girdles unto the merchant" (v. 24). This provided extra income for the family. And in modern times I have seen a little extra income help many a family get off the economic treadmill.

11. In summary, "She looketh well to the ways of her household, and [as you would know] eateth not the bread of idleness" (v. 27). She exercises loving surveillance over the attitudes, words and actions of the household. The home as well as every other unit of society needs supervision. So in Solomon's portrait of the

ideal wife he pictures one who keeps an eye on family life and affairs — an absolute essential of success!

12. Now we note her rewards:

1) She has the joy and gratification of having a successful and honored husband. "Her husband is known in the gates, when he sitteth among the elders of the land" (v. 23). His repute is widespread. In such a man — a companion to herself and a father to her children — a woman should have the greatest delight, and especially if she has done much to make it possible.

2) She has the appreciation and gratitude of her children. "Her children arise up, and call her blessed" (v. 28). They call her blessed because she has blessed them. She deserves it.

3) Her husband applauds her. "Her husband also . . . praiseth her" (v. 28). He appreciatively says, "Many daughters have done virtuously [worthily], but thou excellest them all" (v. 29). No flattery. Just a fact. She earned the approbation.

4) As is true of all meritorious laudations, the praises paid this woman spring from her own deeds. "Let her own works praise her in the gates" (v. 31). Her fruitful life speaks for itself. Just as a tree is known by its fruits, so is a human being. Her fruits declare her industry, ability, devotion and goodness.

Fortunate is the man who has her!

Now I call attention to some concrete examples of which I am personally acquainted. Perhaps you also have observed many.

In this particular family the husband found his work very demanding and gruelling. But unbeknown to him, his wife decided to do something about it. She began to watch her household money with more thought and thrift, and as a result she was able to lay aside some savings week by week. Additionally, as she got a chance to earn some money she did and put it in the secret fund. Several years passed. Then the day came and she asked her husband, "How would you like to buy a farm and move to the country?" "What with?" he inquired. When she told him that she had the money, he at first thought she was joking. But it was so. They bought a farm, and there they lived the rest of their years, enjoying the slower pace in which they made less money but needed less.

Also, there is the woman who began dealing in antiques in her home. She made money. From there she moved into a commercial building and has done well. How well — only she, the Lord and the Internal Revenue Service know, but it is very evident that she has prospered.

And there is the woman who put in a little dress shop. Its growth has been spectacular.

Some sell cosmetics and jewelry from the home. Their accomplishments are to be admired.

And there is another who owns a store that specializes in clothes for children. She has made it pay.

And a little unusual is the woman in the printing business. She, too, has earned her success.

To continue would be superfluous.

In Bible language, "Her price is far above rubies." In view of her worth, Rule Number Nine for a couple includes the wife — *she should do her part.*

THINK ON THESE THINGS

1. What aspects of our future life do we choose for ourselves when we choose a mate?
2. Women take care of many, if not most, of the regular monthly expenditures (food, etc.). What can be done in your family to show appreciation for the woman's role in wise handling of the family's resources? Let her know her efforts are appreciated!
3. What role can the woman in your family have in increasing the family income?
4. Analyze all monthly expenditures. Which shopping habits (food, clothing, etc.) can be altered to economize?
5. What about menu planning, cash only purchases, putting up the credit cards, etc.? Will these or other plans help the most?
6. What adverb describes the manner in which the "Worthy Woman" of Proverbs worked?
7. What did the "Worthy Woman" of Proverbs do with some of the money she accumulated?
8. The "Worthy Woman" of Proverbs is no "door mat," or "yes lady." Neither does she eat bon-bons on a satin pillow. What areas of the "Worthy Woman's" career can be duplicated today?

THIRTEEN

Rich or Super-Rich?

It IS INTERESTING and revealing to size up the people who have prospered. There are reasons. No accident. They have qualities which pushed them up the financial ladder. The aforementioned rules for prosperity in the previous chapters shed light on the traits of those who have achieved it. Without being redundant, I wish to specify those attributes and elaborate further:

1. Every self-made, well-off person is a work horse of a man or woman. No sluggard. The get-aheaders have learned well that in nature's plan, provided by the Creator, man's survival is predicated on work (Genesis 3:19). They are not time watchers; instead, overtime is one of their stocks in trade. Did you ever notice how many executives carry brief cases home at night?

Why do they do it? Some for money. Some for the ego satisfaction. Some because they want to climb to the top. But with most of them the inducement to work for material reward or earthly glory is lost in the joy of labor for its own sake. The hard worker is obsessed with the mere zest of his activity.

2. They know that their welfare is their own responsibility. Not the company's for which they work. Not the community's. Not the government's. They realize that they, with God's help, determine what they will be, how

far they will go and what they will have. The Bible tells us: "A sower went forth to sow" — individual responsibility (Matthew 13:4). "And the recompense of a man's hands shall be rendered unto him" — the compensation of a man's own hands, not the fruit of another's hands (Proverbs 12:14).

That others can aid or hinder is conceded, but triumphant people overcome the hindrances.

3. Furthermore, they definitely intended to get ahead. A singleness of purpose kept them on the road that led to their goal. Success begins with a purpose. This is clearly set forth in the Scriptures:

> To every thing there is a season, and a time to every purpose under the heaven: . . . a time to plant . . . a time to gather . . . a time to get.
>
> Ecclesiastes 3:1-6

In every success story there is a determined man or woman, bent on rising above the ordinary. This force of will to be or to achieve is actually the first sign of greatness and the starting point in a successful career.

> *Singleness of purpose is one of the chief essentials for success in life, no matter what may be one's aim.*
>
> *John D. Rockefeller, Jr.*

4. Another very pronounced characteristic of the financially triumphant is the saving habit. Thrifty. They have gone to the ant and learned: "Go to the ant . . . consider her ways, and be wise . . . provideth her meat in the summer, and gathereth her food in the harvest" (Proverbs 6:6-8).

One sure mark of the future well-to-do person is that he manages his finances so that his revenues always exceed his expenditures. He begins to lay a little aside, almost as soon as he begins to earn.

> *The first thing a man should learn to do is to save his money. By saving his money he promotes thrift — the most valued of all habits. Thrift is the great fortune-maker . . . not only develops the fortune, but it develops, also, the man's character.*
>
> *Andrew Carnegie*

5. Moreover, the get-aheaders have drive. It relentlessly impels them toward their objective. This is one of the reasons why the "old boys with no chance" make it to the top. They come from the backwoods, the plains, the mountains, the villages and the cities. It is not where they are from but what is in them that makes the difference.

Truly —

> *The world belongs to the energetic.*
>
> *Ralph Waldo Emerson*

No! It does not belong to the sluggard who desires and has nothing, but to the diligent who is made affluent (Proverbs 13:4).

6. An additional trait — they think. Good judgment seems to be a part of them. They see not the beginning but the end.

> O that they were wise, that they understood this, that they would consider their latter end!
>
> Deuteronomy 32:29

A universal trait of wealthy people is that they ordinarily look before they leap. Their large accumulations of wealth are the result of initiative and ability to organize, and even more — their judgment, without which the other qualities would produce only meager rewards. Initiative moves men, but unless there is accurate thinking the move may be in the wrong direction.

7. Definitely, the successful are not gullible. They place more credence in evidence than in what some person says. The Scriptures make a distinction in the naive and the judicious:

> The simple believeth every word; but the prudent man looketh well to his going.
>
> Proverbs 14:15

Years ago I heard grandfather tell of inspecting some land for sale. He and the owner walked across some bottom ground adjacent to a running stream. He noticed mud and silt rings more than waist high on the trees. This prodded him to inquire: "Does the creek ever overflow and cover this land?" When the owner said, "No," grandfather further asked, "Well, what are those rings doing on those trees?" "Oh, that dirt on the trees," replied the owner, "it was left by the hogs rubbing up against them." After they got back to the house the would-be-seller said, "Think you might be interested in buying my farm?" "No, I guess not," replied grandfather, "but I surely would like to get a start of those hogs."

8. In meeting the prosperous, we also meet the self-confident people. Confidence drove from them the demon of fear which is always ready to whisper: "You can't do it." "Too hard." "If it's such a good idea, why hasn't somebody else done it?" "If you don't try, you won't fail." "Once poor, always poor." "Accept the fate of lesser talent." However, the successful people disarmed the demon by believing they could succeed. They found

hidden forces within themselves which confidence awakened and put to work for them.

9. To the unbeaten there is no failure. What others call failure is to them only temporary defeat. Give up? Never! The world can knock them down, but they have a way of getting back on their feet. Bravery is truly an essential trait. And heroic.

When plans go amiss and losses come — whatever they are — we need to find something to be thankful for and take courage. For courage is in God's plan for man: "Be thou strong and very courageous . . . that thou mayest prosper . . ." (Joshua 1:7).

10. What's more, they learn from their mistakes. This is proof they are wise; however, the foolish refuse to learn and thereby bring upon themselves poverty, as the Bible states:

> Poverty and shame shall be to him that refuseth instruction: but he that regardeth reproof shall be honored.
>
> Proverbs 13:18

Even a fox learns from his blunders — why can't every man be that smart? A fox, a devourer of fowl and small animals, learns to keep his distance from one little creature — the skunk. One lesson is all he needs. But people, poor foolish creatures, how they get taken in! Again and again!

11. Additionally, successful people are persistent. They have a steadfast and unmoveable temperament, a prerequisite of success in every field. One thing about them, they last, they never quit. They know how to hang in there. One of them has in his office a painting of a monkey holding on to a fragile limb swinging over

a deep canyon. At one side of the picture are the words, *Hang in There*. In another's office there is on the wall this plaque:

> If thou faint in the day of adversity, thy strength is small.
>
> Proverbs 24:10

12. Generally speaking, wealthy men and women are honest and dependable. At least, I have found them that way. Some say, "With all their money they can afford to be." But when they were poor they felt that they couldn't afford not to be honest, for it was contrary to their nature and likewise to the laws of success to be a cheat. In addition to their own moral conviction, they know that there is no way to be big if one is internally possessed with the littleness of dishonesty. They may not know that this is in the Bible, but they have learned to abide by the principle anyway:

> Ye shall not steal, neither deal falsely, neither lie one to another.
>
> Leviticus 19:11

13. The prosperous realize that prosperity has a price tag and that only those who are willing to pay the cost can have it. Nothing comes free — not even failure, for it, too, requires even higher and more galling payments in the long run than success.

The triumphant go the extra mile. They put out more than is required just to get by. "Good enough" is not enough for them. They go farther, work harder and do better than the average. This is one way to get ahead: *go the extra mile* which the average person will not do. They are active planners, active workers, active sacrificers and active disciplinarians. Diligence is one of the reasons for their affluence:

> He becometh poor that dealeth with a slack hand: but the hand of the diligent maketh rich.
>
> Proverbs 10:4

With such qualities, no wonder they prosper!

THE SUPER-RICH

Now meet the people who are a greater financial success. They have the necessary traits to accumulate wealth, mentioned in this chapter and in the preceding chapters, plus more, much more. For there is a difference between Financial Success and Financial Accumulation. Some people have erred in measuring Financial Success as Financial $ucce$$ — just dollars. This is *financial accumulation* but not *financial success*. Making money and saving it is not necessarily a success story. The real achievement comes from what is done with it. This is true of an individual, and it is just as true of a church or any other group supported by contributions. It is harder to wisely handle money than it is to efficiently amass it.

Unequivocally, the super-rich are the people who have done more than follow the divine principles of accumulating riches. Their concept of wealth stretches beyond getting it. They are super-rich because they are more than rich, because they recognize the Super-One from whom all wealth comes and follow His guiding principles in using it properly. This gives a *richness more valuable than money.* Note these beautiful attributes:

1. They are aware that this is God's world and that He has the right to bless. "Give us this day our daily bread" (Matthew 6:11). The prayer shows faith in divine intervention in man's affairs. Man can plant the wheat, but it is God that gives the qualities that make it produce.

2. They recognize that all material blessings come from the Creator. "Every good gift and every perfect gift is from above, and cometh down from the Father" (James 1:17). Man can only alter, cultivate and appropriate that which has been created.

3. The super-rich remember that it is the Lord "that giveth thee power to get wealth" (Deuteronomy 8:18). The gift has come in many ways: life, a place to work in His world, the working of nature, intelligence, skills, knowledge, energy, unseen blessings and the instructions for the attainment of prosperity. This is humbling.

4. They realize that God can separate man from his wealth: First, by allowing death — ". . . this night thy soul shall be required of thee: then whose shall those things be, which thou hast provided" (Luke 12:20)? Second, by permitting bankruptcy. This was Job's fate; however, "in all this Job sinned not, nor charged God foolishly" (Job 1:22). With such an attitude, we can understand how Job made a financial comeback stronger than ever.

5. They have given to the Lord and they have received in return. Indeed, they are not followers of slot machine religion — put in a quarter hoping to get back $10.00 — because their motives are high and unselfish. Plainly put, giving to get is greed, and surely God is not going to reward it. Yet, God will give to those who

honor Him and give unselfishly. For God has promised: "But seek ye first the kingdom of God, and his righteousness; and all these things [material things] shall be added unto you" (Matthew 6:33). "Honor the Lord with thy substance, and with the firstfruits of all thine increase: so shall thy barns be filled with plenty, and thy presses shall burst out with new wine" (Proverbs 3:9,10). Says it. Seek first the kingdom. Honor the Lord with firstfruits. First! First! Put the Lord first! This being true, no one can be more than a superficial success who does not have this more meaningful view of wealth.

Do I hear it said, "I have known people to give freely, but have not prospered bountifully?" Yes. But now let me ask, "Did they follow the God-given rules for prosperity as well as give? Did they do both?" God has promised to increase the prosperity of those who honor Him by giving of their substance. But He has also specified that they are to obey His laws to obtain substance. It is like the man who prays for his daily bread. The prayer does not eliminate the need to break the soil, plant the seed, cultivate the crop and harvest it.

6. The richer-than-money people are cognizant that they can't take anything with them into the eternal realm. "For we brought nothing into this world, and it is certain we can carry nothing out" (I Timothy 6:7). When they are gone, the wealth is left behind.

They know that the wealth was never really theirs in the first place. It has always belonged to God and always will. *Man is just a steward.* And only for a short time. And when the time is up, they know that they will have to account for their stewardship. This is most evident from the Parable of the Talents. Remember — the "talents" in the parable were sums of money, not abilities. Three persons were given different amounts. It is noteworthy and perhaps shocking to some that the one given the least (one coin) turned out to be the hoarder. Nevertheless, he had to account for what was given him, as did the others with more, and was condemned for the misuse of his money (Matthew 25:24-30). So, whether man has little or much, he is accountable for his stewardship. And it is faithful stewardship that gives gold a more golden luster and a greater value.

While a person cannot take his riches with him, he can send them on ahead of him. It is called "lay up for yourselves treasures in heaven" (Matthew 6:20).

7. Appreciative of their blessings, they ask, "What shall I render unto the Lord for all his benefits toward me" (Psalms 116:12)? Man renders unto the Lord by using wealth as the Lord has taught. He has stated that in just giving to "the least of these my brethren, ye have done it unto me" (Matthew 24:40). And just a cup of cold water can be of great significance. He teaches:

1) Use prosperity to support yourself and your family. A divine injunction! This is so basic that a refusal to do it puts one in a class that is considered worse than infidels (I Timothy 5:8). To do this effectively requires thought. To provide too much for children may make them irresponsible dependents, playboys and playgirls. To give them too little may cause them to resent you. I have seen it happen both ways. Concerning the latter, a fairly prosperous man was too saving to own a car when his children were growing up. All the neighbors had one or more. His attitude did more than pinch pen-

nies — it pinched the kids. As a result, they disrespected him and later denied the very religion he sought to instill in them.

2) Also, it is suitable and moral to leave an inheritance for children, provided the parents think it will help them rather than hurt them. It is Biblical: the parents ought to lay up for the children (II Corinthians 12:14). It can be a head start. Let's hope it is not a ball and chain.

3) Give to the poor. "He hath given to the poor" (Psalms 112:9), because he had it and because he had more than monetary competence — he had mercy. A full purse should never diminish the size of your heart. Giving to the underprivileged is more than sympathy; it is sympathy in action, which is kindness.

4) Assist the needy. "Give to him that needeth" (Ephesians 4:28). The passage further states that this is one of the reasons for working and having. It puts capital on the move for good whereby it flows into the empty pantries, barren walls and sickrooms of the destitute.

5) Support widows and orphans. This is such a bighearted and compassionate deed that the Bible calls it pure and undefiled religion (James 1:17). A religion without a heart is empty and vain, and so is a heartless rich man. He is only a SUCCE$$, just a dollar success, no genuine success.

6) Give to the church and other worthy and helpful causes. Here is a Scripture directed to the church at Corinth that relates giving to prosperity: "Upon the first day of the week let every one of you lay by him in store,

as God hath prospered him" (I Corinthians 16:2). The passage teaches weekly giving — not weakly giving — based on prosperity.

In the second letter to the same church we see that giving comes freely when there is "first a willing mind" and a giving of self (8:12,5). Indeed, he who gives self will not deny his money. It is then that he knows the luxury of having through the luxury of giving.

It is this attitude toward gold and the giving of it that gives one the golden blessings which are more precious than gold.

Jesus said:

> Freely ye have received, freely give.
> Matthew 10:8

It is not what we keep but what we give that is ours. What we give to others and to the Master's cause is ours and ours forever. Everything else perishes.

Money definitely has a place in our lives and in the world. Truly, the prosperous person who follows the divine principles of handling wealth is super-rich. May you have plenty, and may you have the wisdom to use it properly.

> For unto whomsoever much is given of him shall be much required.
> Luke 12:48

Believing "this is the way, walk ye in it."

THINK ON THESE THINGS

1. What success traits do you already possess?
2. What success traits do you need to further develop?
3. Why do most prosperous people work hard?
4. How was the ant used to teach a lesson?
5. Compare the price of poverty versus the price of prosperity?
6. What is the real difference between "rich" and "super-rich"?
7. Why is generosity towards God not always enough to make one financially prosperous?
8. Why do Christians need to make money and be financially prosperous?